THE SOCIAL FRAMEWORK

OF

THE AMERICAN ECONOMY

AN INTRODUCTION TO ECONOMICS

THE SOCIAL FRAMEWORK
OF
THE AMERICAN ECONOMY

AN INTRODUCTION TO ECONOMICS

BY

J. R. HICKS
STANLEY JEVONS PROFESSOR OF POLITICAL ECONOMY
IN THE UNIVERSITY OF MANCHESTER

AND

ALBERT GAILORD HART
PROFESSOR OF ECONOMICS, COLUMBIA UNIVERSITY

OXFORD UNIVERSITY PRESS
NEW YORK   1945

Copyright 1945 by Oxford University Press, New York, Inc.

This is an American edition, based on J. R. Hicks'
The Social Framework: An Introduction to Economics,
first published in 1942.

Fifth Printing, June 1947

PRINTED IN THE UNITED STATES OF AMERICA

CONTENTS

PART IV. *The Social Output*

PREFACE

I have written this book because I have come to hold a particular point of view about the right way to arrange economics for elementary study.

Until lately the problem of how to begin the study of economics reduced itself to a dilemma: either one might begin with economic theory—which meant in practice the theory of supply and demand—or one might begin with descriptive economics, the practical problems of industry and labor. Now there were serious objections against each course. To begin with the theory of value meant starting off with problems whose significance it is difficult for the beginner to realize, and on a field where generalizations which will stand up to criticism are singularly difficult to attain. Descriptive economics, on the other hand, taken without a sufficient grounding in theory, is inevitably either a dull collection of facts or, alternatively, a discussion of practical policies which may be lively enough, but which it is hard to raise much above the intellectual level of political propaganda. In practice, whichever of these solutions was adopted, some of these difficulties were incurred. The student who pursued a long course of study would of course find his way round them in the end, though not without some waste of time. But those people whose acquaintance with economics was confined to a one-year course (and they are a large proportion of all students of the subject) were either sent away thoroughly bored—if their teachers had followed the austerer path—or, in the other event, they were left with nothing but ready-made opinions on a few topical issues.

As a result of the developments in economic knowledge which have taken place during recent years, we are now (I believe) in a position to resolve this dilemma, and to do so by something better than a mere compromise between the existing alternatives. It is now possible to mark out a preliminary stage in economic study, which is wholly concerned with topics which are obviously interesting and important, and which is yet systematic enough to give some of the mental discipline necessary for study on a scientific level. At the same time this stage involves very little of that process of *abstraction* which is such a snare in the elementary stages of the theory of value. The ideas involved are simple and obviously sensible; the discipline is provided by the considerable demands which are made for care and patience in putting them together.

This change has come about because the chapters on definitions, which formed so indigestible a portion of the old textbooks, have been kindled into life by the work of economic statisticians, and also by some of the newer developments of economic theory. They have grown into a distinct branch of economics, a branch which is being pursued with very special success at the present time, and which is, nevertheless, particularly suited to serve as an introduction to the science in general. If we want a name for it, it might be described as Social Accounting, for it is nothing else but the accounting of the whole community or nation, just as Private Accounting is the accounting of the individual firm.

The greater part of this book is taken up with the study of Social Accounting; but in suggesting that this is probably the best way to begin the study of economics, I am not of course claiming that it can replace the conventional elementary theory and elementary applied economics. I would indeed claim that, in these days of shortened courses, a student who begins with Social Accounting will learn something useful and something worth learning, even if his studies are broken off at an early stage. But my main contention is that the other topics should come afterwards, after the groundwork of Social Accounting has been mastered. I hope and believe that when a beginner has mastered the substance of this book, he will be able to turn to the theory of value with some idea of what he wants to get from it; and that seems to be an essential preliminary to getting anything worth having.

Later on—but perhaps it will have to wait until quieter times—I plan myself to write an outline of the theory of value, in a form which would serve as a sequel to this book. And I should also like to write a further sequel, giving a similar elementary treatment of Money and Finance.

I have a number of acknowledgments to make. I believe that the first idea of developing an approach to economics along these lines came to me when taking pupils who were attending the elementary lectures of Professor Pigou. Not having had the advantage of attending those lectures myself, I cannot say how far the further development of my ideas would meet with his approval. Nevertheless, I should like to thank him for planting the seed in my mind.

I have to thank Sir Hubert Henderson for finally resolving a prolonged indecision about the book's title.

My other obligations are mainly statistical. Being myself a very amateurish statistician, I should never have dared to venture as far as I have done on to this field, if it had not been for the advice and criticism which were constantly available to me, first from my wife and secondly from my colleague Dr. Singer. Finally, over two of the chapters which cost me the greatest difficulty to write (xiv and xvii), I had the great good fortune to get into contact with Mr. T. Barna, of the London School of Economics, who generously put at my disposal work of his own which gave much better answers to some of the questions I was asking than I could have provided myself. My acknowledgments to Mr. Barna are recorded in detail in those chapters, and in the Appendix.

J. R. H.

Manchester
May 1942

PREFACE TO THE AMERICAN EDITION

In commissioning the preparation of this American version of *The Social Framework*, Professor Hicks described the job as one of 'translation.' In accordance with his very broad construction, I have taken translation to include not merely Americanizing spelling, idiom, and sentence structure, and replacing some illustrations, but also bringing the book more or less into the same relation to the American literature and official statistics which the original edition has to corresponding British materials. A particular effort has been made to create a bridge between the discussion of the economic logic of national income and the concrete materials of the Department of Commerce.

The division into parts and chapters, and the general sequence of topics within the chapters, conforms to the British edition. Except for the wealth statistics of Chapter x (for which I can see no satisfactory American equivalent), American statistics have been used throughout. In accordance with American tradition, the tables are rather more fully itemized and described than their British equivalents.

Weaving in the American material has necessitated substantial changes of arrangement and emphasis in the central group of chapters on Social Output (xi through xvii), and in particular bringing the concept of factor cost to the surface in Chapter xiii and amplifying that chapter. In reaching an agreement on these chapters, Professor Hicks has been at some pains to avoid putting me in the position of expounding views I do not fully share; and except for a few

terminological points on which I have surrendered rather
mild preferences, they represent my best judgment as well
as his. I believe a careful reader will find no conflicts between
the two editions.

No American teacher of economics can have failed to sense
the 'dilemma' which Professor Hicks has aimed to solve
through this book. A 'theoretical' introduction means inviting
the student to acquire a parlor accomplishment, which lacks
meaning for want of realistic knowledge. An 'institutional' introduction ordinarily means inviting the student to inform
himself about facts and opinions, without enabling him to
integrate the facts or criticize the opinions systematically.
The dilemma is one example of the superficially competitive
relation between the institutional and theoretical approaches,
which basically are complementary. The solution of using
national income to give order to an institutional introduction
has been advocated in discussions of teaching problems in
the *American Economic Review* and elsewhere; and the usefulness of income and product measures in interpreting
United States war experience testifies to its soundness.

A. G. H.

Chicago
June 1945

THE SOCIAL FRAMEWORK

OF

THE AMERICAN ECONOMY

AN INTRODUCTION TO ECONOMICS

ECONOMIC FACTS AND ECONOMIC THEORY

1. WHAT ECONOMICS IS ABOUT

Economics—the subject which we are going to study in this book, and in the successors which will (I hope) one day follow it—is a science, one of the branches of that great systematic study of the world we live in which we call Science with a capital S. The division of Science into sciences—physics, chemistry, biology, physiology, and so on—is largely a matter of convenience; we group together in a science those particular special studies which are conveniently pursued together and pursued by the same people. This means that we cannot tell where the frontiers of a particular science will prove to be until we have developed that science; and we need not expect that these frontiers will always be found in the same place. Even between the two most highly developed of the natural sciences, physics and chemistry, the boundary is distinctly fluctuating. Chemistry deals with those aspects of the world which are conveniently studied by chemists; economics deals with those aspects which are conveniently studied by economists.

All the same, within the broad field of the sciences in general, economics belongs, without any doubt, to a particular sub-group; it belongs to the Human Sciences, the sciences which are concerned with human behavior. There are other human sciences besides economics: there is psychology, and there is politics (the science of government); there is perhaps also sociology, a less definite science dealing with such things as religion and the family. Anthropology deals with

1

the structure of the societies which our complacent grand-
fathers called 'primitive.' History and geography deal with the
same subject matter as these sciences, though arranging it in
different patterns. All these touch on economics, so that the
student of economics is well advised to maintain a certain
interest in them. From his point of view politics is probably
the most important—the dividing line which separates it from
economics is the hardest to draw. The close connection between economics and politics is illustrated in the older name
for economics—Political Economy.

Provisionally, we may say that the particular aspect of
human behavior which is dealt with by economics is the behavior of human beings in business. Economics is the science
which deals with business affairs. But if we allow ourselves
to say this, then we must be clear that business is to be understood in a wide sense. When a housewife goes into a shop
to buy some bacon, the resulting transaction is undoubtedly a
business transaction from the point of view of the shopkeeper,
and so would fall within our definition of the subject matter of
economics. We should not so naturally regard it as a business
transaction from the housewife's point of view. But once economics has undertaken the study of this piece of behavior,
the transaction has to be looked at scientifically, that is to say,
from all sides; economics has to pay just as much attention to
the housewife's side of the bargain as to the shopkeeper's.
Buying the bacon is an economic question just as much as
selling it.

To take some other examples. When men or women are
paid wages to work in a factory, their employment is obviously a business question from the point of view of the employer. Consequently, it comes into economics, but economics
has to consider the worker's point of view as well as the employer's. The payment of taxes on profits is again obviously
a business question; economics has to consider the payment
of taxes from all sides, looking at it from the standpoint of

the firms and private people who pay the taxes, from that of the government which receives revenue from the taxes, and from that of the people whose wages and other incomes are paid by the government out of this revenue. Once we make these extensions—and they are absolutely necessary extensions —the subject matter of economics loses most of the narrowness it might appear to have at first sight. The problems of profit-making business have been much more important at some periods of history than at others. But economic problems have always been of the utmost importance, and it is safe to predict that they always will be. Although there are wide stretches of human experience (the whole fields of art and religion, for example) on which economics has nothing, or nothing fundamental, to say, economic activities do occupy a large part of the life of nearly everyone, and are bound to do so. Economic science endeavors to study these activities scientifically; it has in fact made better progress in the application of scientific methods to the study of human conduct than has been made by the other social sciences. The study of economics can, therefore, take us a considerable way towards a general understanding of human society, that is, of men's behavior to one another.

2. The Sources of Economic Information

The method of modern economic investigation is the same as the method of all science. Economics studies facts, and seeks to arrange the facts in such ways as make it possible to draw conclusions from them. As always, it is the arrangement which is the delicate operation. Facts, arranged in the right way, speak for themselves; unarranged, they are as dead as mutton. One of the main things we have to learn is how to arrange our facts properly.

Where does the economist get his facts? It might be thought that, since the object of economics is to study human conduct in business affairs, the simplest way of proceeding

would be to go to the people engaged in business affairs and
to ask them questions. But a moment's reflection will show
that this is not as promising a line as it looks. Even if we
are lucky, and the particular man we select is willing to tell
us about the things which seem to him to be important (in
practice even that is far from certain), he is unlikely to be
able to tell us about other things which may be more important from our point of view. If we ask him about something which he did six months ago he is not very likely to
be able to remember. Yet that may be just the question we
want answered. It is very difficult to get systematic information in this sort of way.

An improvement upon the simple method of interviewing
is the questionnaire. If a large number of people are asked
the same set of questions, some will not reply, some will
make guesses or answer at random, some will reply seriously.
By looking over all the replies together, it may be possible
to sort out the replies which are significant from those which
are not. The method of questionnaires is successful only
where those questioned can be persuaded to take an interest
in giving full and accurate answers. Occasionally this interest
is secured by paying for the information. Sometimes the appeal is to a sense of public duty—the mainstay of official census
inquiries. Sometimes the appeal is to the sense of fun of the
person questioned, and to his desire for social prestige. But
the difficulty of getting full and accurate replies, coupled
with the high cost of assembling and tabulating the answers,
limits the amount of information which can be collected spe-
cifically to help the economist analyze society. For the most
part our information comes from another source.

This other source of information consists in facts which
have been collected for other purposes than for use by economists, but which can be used by economists. Naturally, since
these facts have been brought together for other purposes
than ours, there are large parts of these collections which

are, from our point of view, sheer rubbish. But it is a perfectly feasible (though laborious) task to separate out from the rubbish the information we want.

Large quantities of facts, potentially interesting to the economist, are collected nowadays by business organizations; but the most important collections are those made by governments. Modern governments collect stupendously large quantities of facts, occasionally from pure love of knowledge, but more often for the pedestrian reason that they need these facts for the ordinary running of public affairs. At any rate, in time of peace a large proportion of these facts are published, occasionally (again) in order to inform the public, but more often because published information is actually more easily accessible to public servants themselves than information which is not published. A government which employs many thousands of people has the greatest difficulty in keeping its left hand informed of what its right hand is doing; publicity makes for efficiency in administration. It is a purely incidental advantage that it provides the economist with valuable material at the same time.

When using this administrative information, it is essential to remember how it is compiled, and why; otherwise one may easily go astray. For example, when the government publishes a statement that so many persons have been unemployed on a certain date, the precise figure which is given will depend upon the definition of unemployment used—whether people who have only been out of work for two or three days are counted as unemployed, and so on. It occasionally happens that the definition of *unemployed* is changed slightly; when this occurs, the figures given may change without there being any real change in unemployment. The definitions of unemployment which are used in the unemployment figures of different countries do in fact differ very considerably indeed; so that the international comparison of unemployment is a very ticklish matter. This sort of difficulty is one for which we have constantly to be on the watch.

3. REGULAR SOURCES AVAILABLE IN THE UNITED STATES

Governments collect and publish material on all sorts of subjects. From the economic point of view, the most useful parts of the collection are the 'time series,' which give information on a comparable basis for a number of different dates, enabling us to trace social changes. Among the more important series for the United States are the following:

A. *The Census of Population.* The United States Census is a constitutional necessity—an interesting example of the way in which economic data arise as a by-product of politics—because it is the basis of representation in Congress. Consequently a census has been taken every ten years, beginning in 1790. Besides counting the number of people in each part of the country, the census-takers record people's ages, countries of birth, family status, occupations, housing arrangements, and innumerable other facts. The 1940 census included a study of incomes. By using data on 'vital statistics' (births and deaths) and migrations between censuses, reliable population estimates for intermediate dates can be made. Similarly, employment data are used to fill in figures on occupations for years between censuses.

B. *The Censuses of Agriculture, Manufactures, etc.* Certain questions about economic life were early included in the Census. As time went on, inquiries began to be made between regular census years. The census of agriculture has been taken at five-year intervals for some time. The census of manufactures was taken every ten years 1849-99, every five years 1899-1919, every two years 1919-39. Other lines of inquiry have gradually developed until the greater part of American business has been brought under periodic investigation.

C. *Production Data.* Mining activity has long been recorded by the U.S. Bureau of Mines; the series for coal production goes back to 1821. Since 1919, the Federal Reserve System has built up detailed measures of manufacturing activity. Railway and water traffic, electric power production, etc., are also measured.

D. *Trade Data.* Foreign trade has been recorded for centuries by governments; relatively full American series go back to the beginning of the federal government in 1789. Domestic trade data are collected on a vast scale by the Department of Commerce and Federal Reserve.

E. *Employment and Wage Data.* Unlike most European countries, where trade unions have comprehensive records, the United States has only recently begun to develop a rich fund of labor statistics. For the inter-war period (1919-40) the Bureau of Labor Statistics has indexes of employment, wages, working hours, and payrolls in manufacturing; and for dates since 1929 there are respectable figures for many other branches of the economy. Social Security records are rapidly increasing our knowledge in this field.

F. *Price Data.* Current prices of all sorts of things are under continuous study at the Bureau of Labor Statistics, Department of Commerce, and Federal Reserve. By use of old newspaper files, price series have been extended backwards for decades.

G. *Financial Data.* Data on the receipts and expenditures of the government, the supply of money, the working of the banking system, etc., are direct by-products of government operations. The Securities and Exchange Commission keeps track of dealings in new and old stocks and bonds, and estimates the flow of savings.

H. *Special Inquiries.* Occasionally bodies of data are assembled by special inquiries which may or may not be followed up later to yield time series. Sometimes these are attached to the Census, like the unemployment census of 1930 and the income census of 1940; sometimes they are separate enterprises, like the Financial Survey of Urban Housing (1933-4) and Study of Consumer Purchases (1935-6).

The enormous mass of data available on a monthly or weekly basis can be found for the most part in the *Survey of Current Business;* more detail on special subjects appears in *Federal Reserve Bulletin, Monthly Labor Review, Social Security Bulletin,* and *Bulletin of the Treasury Department.* The still greater mass of annual data is conveniently assembled in *Statistical Abstract of the United States.* On some topics for which unofficial series are the main sources (life insurance, for instance), these publications include the unofficial figures.

There are numerous other sources of economic information, but these are the main regular types, which give us similar information for a large number of different dates. In themselves they comprise an immense body of material—when it is put together with similar material from other countries it is enough to fill a library of considerable size. Even so, there are many economic questions we might like to have answered whose answers cannot be found within this material; that is why some part of the time of some economists is properly spent in collecting additional information, by questionnaires and so on. But the questions which can be answered from the existing material, more or less satisfactorily, are numerous and important; however, we can only begin to answer them properly if we go about doing so in the right way.

4. QUANTITATIVE AND QUALITATIVE INFORMATION

It should not be inferred from the foregoing inventory that economic knowledge consists exclusively of figures. On the contrary, it consists largely of *qualitative* information. Without this qualitative information, furthermore, the quantitative information contained in our statistics could not be interpreted.

Some examples of needed qualitative information will clarify the point. To begin with, some notion of the common patterns of thought of the people in our society is essential to the economist. He must also know the fundamentals of the law of property; the general methods of organization by which the groups of people who act jointly as firms or as households are held together; the characteristic fallacies committed by people in thinking about their private affairs; the types of 'interferences' in economic life which government finds it necessary or expedient to enter upon.

The 'institutional' approach to economics involved in qualitative inquiries along these lines is often represented as an alternative to the 'theoretical' approach traditional among economists. This apparent conflict is a fraud. The two approaches are both necessary, and complement each other—for reasons which will shortly appear.

5. THE STAGES OF ACQUIRING ECONOMIC KNOWLEDGE

There are four stages in the process of acquiring economic knowledge which can be distinguished from one another, so much so that they are often regarded as separate departments of the science. But we should be quite clear about the sense in which they are separate departments. It is not that the problems they deal with are different—the same problem is often handed on from one to another of them. It is merely that they do different parts of the work of solution.

First of all, there is the stage or department which is called *Economic Theory*. The basic function of economic theory is to prepare the questions which we want to ask of the facts. It is absolutely useless to study a mountain of facts without knowing, first of all, and very precisely and clearly, what one is looking for. We start from common sense, and the broad lines of obvious information which we derive from our daily experience; we set it in order, so as to get our questions into a useful form. It is only when we have done some preparation of this sort that we can approach the facts with any prospect of getting something significant out of them.

At the second stage, we make our approach to the facts. After we have decided what questions we want to ask, we have to pick out from the whole mass of economic information described above those parts which have something to tell us about the question in hand. Then, when we have made that selection, we have to examine the information, and find out exactly what it means. This last is a very important step, as can be seen from the example of the unemployment figures which was given earlier. We have to examine how the figures were collected, and what definitions were used; we have to ask whether these definitions are the same as those we found convenient in our economic theory; if not, what adjustments can be made, on one side or the other, to allow for the difference. What is chiefly involved in this second stage is a knowledge of the material out of which we are to get our results.

In the organization of the subject, this second stage is reckoned as a part of *Economic Statistics*. The word Statistics is used in two senses—in the plural, to denote the numerical facts, the figures, which are the material we have been discussing; in the singular, to denote the method of handling that material. Here we are concerned with statistics in the singular.

The third stage is also a part of economic statistics. When we have got our information sorted out, we shall nearly always find that it is not complete; there are matters about which we should desire to have information, but unfortunately it has not been collected in the way we want. To some extent it is possible to remedy these defects by making guesses or estimates; a good deal of progress has been made in answering the delicate question what sorts of guesses are reasonably safe, and what are not. This same problem of how to make reasonable estimates arises in many other sciences; we can, to some extent, borrow the methods which they have developed for this purpose. But a good deal of care has to be exercised in doing so.

Finally, in the fourth stage, we have to arrange the facts so as to bring out the answers to our questions as well as we can. This is the stage which is usually known as *Applied* or *Descriptive Economics.* Since, as we have seen, the most useful sorts of facts are those which give us similar information for different dates, it is inevitable that the study of Applied Economics should come very close to that of Economic History. Indeed, it is nearly true to say that Economic History is just the Applied Economics of earlier ages; Applied Economics is concerned with the Economic History of the contemporary world.

6. THE NECESSITY OF ECONOMIC THEORY

In this volume, we shall be concerned entirely with the first and last of these four stages: *theory* for the purpose of clearing our minds and sorting out the questions, *applied economics* to the extent that we shall give some illustrations of the sorts of answers we get to our questions when they are applied to recent history, particularly to the history of the United States and Britain between 1920 and 1939. Economic knowledge is discovered, as we have seen, by co-operation between all the four stages, each of them passing on its difficulties to the others. But for purposes of learning what has been discovered, the first and last of the stages—the ones we are going to deal with—are the ones to begin with. Our basic ideas need to be sorted out, before we can begin to think clearly about economic problems; and we have to start as soon as possible to get practice in the application of our theory to actual experience, if only because in the absence of`such practice it is impossible for the theory itself to be properly understood.

The necessity for this preliminary clearing of ideas which we call Economic Theory appears at once if we reflect how many ideas are used in the ordinary practice of business whose significance is not at all directly obvious. Some of these ideas are of a technical character, arising only in some particular industry, such as shoe making or cotton manufacture; questions of technique are not in themselves of direct interest to the economist, although of course if he desires to make a special study of some particular kind of manufacture, he will probably need to learn something about its technique. The ideas with which economics is concerned are chiefly those which arise not in connection with one industry only, but with most or all industries; such ideas as 'capital,' 'income,' and 'cost' arise in all business problems—these are the sort of ideas we have particularly to study. One of the main purposes of economic theory is to clear our minds about such terms as these. It turns out to be a more complicated matter than might at first sight be supposed. For one thing, these terms were originally invented by business men, for business purposes; but, as we have seen, the economist has to study the business world from a wider point of view than that of the business man. Consequently it is necessary for him not only to understand the business use of these terms, but also to appreciate their wider social significance. Further, when we try to work out this social significance, we find that all these ideas are very closely connected. It is impossible to understand 'income' fully without understanding 'capital' and vice versa. Economic theory, therefore, tends to shape itself into a system of thought, for the questions we want to ask turn out to be interrelated; answering one helps to answer others. We cannot fully understand any one of these ideas unless we have understood its neighbors as well. Answering one question shows us another question to ask, and so on almost indefinitely—but that is, of course, what always happens when we ask any of those key questions about the world which lead to the growth of a science.

In Part I of this book we shall start, as we have to, with

a little theory. Beginning from common sense and everyday experience, we shall sort out our ideas until we have reached a point where we can turn to some of the statistics and hope to learn something from them. In the later Parts we shall run our Theory and our Applied Economics quite closely together.

Part I

THE PRODUCTIVE PROCESS

I

PRODUCTION AND EXCHANGE

1. WORKER, EMPLOYER AND CONSUMER

Economic affairs enter into the life of every one of us, the most important economic activity in the life of the ordinary man being the way he earns his living. People earn their living in all sorts of different ways—by manual work, by brain-work, in factories, in offices, and on farms; in dull ways, in interesting ways. But the thing which is common to all ways of earning one's living is doing work and being paid for doing it. In most countries the majority of people earn their living by working 'for' some particular employer; they receive their payment in the form of a wage or salary (which latter is only a word of Latin origin meaning *wage,* used instead of wage so as to sound grander). But there are some people (it happens with musicians, gardeners, and journalists, for example) who may divide their time between two or three employers. And there are others (shopkeepers, doctors, farmers who deliver milk directly, and so on) who serve quite large numbers of different employers or *customers*—for it is really very much the same thing. Whatever sort of work it is that is done, whatever form the payment for doing it takes, the common element is always there. In order to earn his living a man has to work, and there has to be someone—an employer, or customer, or client—who is prepared to pay him for doing it.

Now why should the employer be prepared to pay? There are in fact several distinct cases. In the first place, an employer may be prepared to pay to have work done for him because the work is directly useful to him personally. A sick man goes to (that is employs) a doctor because he hopes as a result to feel better in health. A householder hires a collector to keep trash from accumulating. A woman patronizes a hairdresser for the sake of 'beauty.' In these instances, and in many others of similar character, the work which is performed provides something which the employer or customer directly wants. Whatever the nature of the want which is to be satisfied, the fact that he is to get something which he wants explains why he is prepared to pay for the work to be performed.

In many other cases the employer is prepared to pay not because the work done is of any use to him personally, but because he expects it to result in something useful to a third person (the Consumer) who will be willing to pay for it. The immediate employer is here nothing but an intermediary; he pays his employee, and the consumer pays him. The wants which are to be satisfied are the consumer's wants; the employer is willing to pay because he expects to be paid by the consumer.

The necessity of having some sort of an employer-intermediary is made evident when one reflects how many workers there are whose work is in itself absolutely useless, though it becomes very useful when it is combined with the work of other people. The typical factory worker, nowadays, is engaged on some small specialized operation, which is only a stage in the making of some part of a useful article, a part like the lace of a shoe or the chain of a bicycle. Unless there are other workers to perform the other stages, and make the other parts, his work is utterly useless. There is no point in doing work of this kind unless there is someone to organize the different operations into a unity. To do this is the work of the employer-intermediary, the business manager or director, the professional employer, who brings together the different people who have the different sorts of skill needed to produce the complete article. Such an employer is not a consumer like the man who employs a doctor or a furnace cleaner;

he is a worker or producer, contributing his own very important share to the process of producing goods which consumers want. Employer and employed are in fact co-operating together in the production of something useful to consumers. They each of them derive their earnings from the payments made by the consumers, who purchase the finished articles they have produced.

Every firm or business consists in essence of a co-operation of workers, organized in some way or another to produce salable products. But the products are not always sold directly to consumers. Very often the product of one firm is sold to another firm, which performs some further operation upon it before it reaches the consumer's hands. Even when a firm has turned out the precise material product which the consumer wants—the jam, the toothpaste, or the newspaper—there is still the further stage of providing it at the place and time where and when it is wanted. To do this is the function of the trader and the shopkeeper, who assist in satisfying people's wants just as much as other workers do. It often happens, on the other hand, that the product turned out by a firm has not yet reached the material form in which the consumer will finally want it. The products of steelworks and spinning mills are only the raw materials of useful articles; they are usually sold to other firms, which use them as ingredients in further production. But even in these cases, although the chain connecting the particular firm with the ultimate consumer may be quite a long one, it is still there. If we take the trouble we can see for ourselves that the ultimate object of the work which is done is to assist in making something which some consumer will want, and will be willing to pay for. That consumer may be near at hand, or he may be at the other end of the earth; still he can always be found if we look for him. It is only because there is a prospect of finding a consumer at the end of the whole process, who will be prepared to pay for something he finds useful or desirable, that people can find employment in industry or in any sort of production at all.

2. SPECIALIZATION AND MUTUAL EXCHANGE

Thus it appears that the whole of the economic activity of humanity (that vast complex of activities which we call the Economic System) consists of nothing else but an immense co-operation of workers or producers to make things and do things which consumers want. When it is described in this way, the economic system may sound quite an admirable thing—perhaps too admirable to agree with our experience of it. But in fact there is nothing necessarily admirable about a co-operation to satisfy the wants of consumers. The wants are usually harmless, but they may be deplorable; the methods of co-operating to satisfy even the most respectable wants are sometimes inefficient and stupid. Yet whether the wants are good or bad, whether production is organized efficiently or not, the description still holds. Economic life is an organization of producers to satisfy the wants of consumers.

Who are these consumers for whom the world is working? To a very large extent they are just the same people as the workers and producers themselves. The same people are workers and producers (or dependents of workers and producers) in one capacity, and consumers in another. The consumer who spends his money upon the product of one industry (a bicycle or a suit of clothes) has earned that money by working in another occupation (say printing or market gardening). The bicycle makers and the clothing and textile workers spend their earnings in turn upon the products of other industries, the workers in these spend their earnings upon other products, and so on. Among the various classes of workers and producers who come into the picture at one or other of these stages, there will be some who will spend some part of their earnings upon the books and newspapers, the vegetables and flowers, which were the products of the printers and market gardeners we started with.

The organization of production and consumption in the modern world is an immensely complicated affair; but if we turn our minds to the way it would be worked out in a simpler state of society, the general nature of the organization is at once apparent. Before the improvements in transportation which have taken place in the last two centuries, the vast majority of the human race lived in fairly self-contained villages, villages which traded with one another in a few kinds of goods, but were in the main self-supporting. In such a village the principle upon which production has to be organized becomes clear at once. The whole thing is a system of exchanges. The farmer uses some part of his produce to satisfy his own wants, but sells some part to his neighbors. With the proceeds of that sale he buys other things which he needs—clothes from the weaver, woodwork from the carpenter, pottery from the potter. The weaver, in his turn, spends some of his time making his own clothes; but he sells most of his produce, using the proceeds to purchase the farmer's milk, or the potter's pots. And so on. 'You do this for me, and I will do that for you.' It is on bargains of this sort that the whole organization rests.

The advantage of organizing economic life in this way arises from the increased efficiency which comes from each person having a job, and sticking to it. 'The jack of all trades is master of none.' Although excessive specialization results in monotonous work, some degree of specialization is needed before any skill can be acquired. Instead of each person working so as to satisfy his own wants alone, which would mean wasting a great deal of time in continually shifting over from one job to another, everyone becomes to some extent a specialist, concentrating on one particular job or small range of jobs. The other things he wants done are done for him by other people, and in exchange for these services he uses his skill in serving them.

The main difference, from this point of view, between the primitive village organization and the economic system of the modern world is that in the modern world specialization has been carried immensely further. The wants of the ordinary person in the twentieth century are catered to by a system of exchanges in which an immensely larger number of people take part. The ordinary worker does not do more than assist in the production of some useful article. He joins together with a large number of other workers in producing something which will be useful to others, or perhaps to some of those he joins with; the things he gets in exchange are themselves the result of extensive, even world-wide, co-operation among producers. The reason for the adoption of this complicated system is still the technical advantage of specialization; subdividing productive processes has increased the efficiency of labor, enabling all sorts of more efficient methods (particularly mechanical methods) to be introduced into production. Nevertheless, in spite of the greater complexity of the specialization involved, the principle remains the same. 'You do this for me, and I will do that for you.'

3. COMPLICATIONS TO THE SYSTEM OF EXCHANGE

(i) *Money.* We have now discovered two different ways of looking at the economic system. On the one hand, we can look upon it as a co-operation of producers to satisfy the wants of consumers; on the other hand, remembering that the producers and consumers are largely the same people, we can look upon it as a system of mutual exchanges. We shall find, as we go on, that it is very useful to have these two different points of view from which to approach our subject. Some things will be clearer from one of these standpoints, some from the other; and we can use one as a check against the other. It will be particularly useful when we come to making the fundamental classifications, which will occupy us in the next two chapters, to be able to check them up from each of these points of view. But before we proceed to that, we ought to satisfy ourselves that our treatment of the system as one of mutual exchanges is really correct, and not subject to qualifications. There are certain difficulties which do undoubt-edly present themselves, and of which we ought to take proper account.

First of all, there is the question of money. Although the ultimate object of anyone who works or produces is to acquire useful things in exchange for his work, the immediate way he gets paid is not in the form of directly useful things, but in the form of money. The printer and journalist do not supply their customers with newspapers, getting bread and meat and clothes in direct exchange; they sell their news-papers for money, and then spend money upon the things they want to buy as consumers. There is an obvious con-venience in this arrangement. It must often happen that the people who supply the printers with clothes do not want to take newspapers to the full value of the clothes. If they had to take payment in newspapers, they would be obliged to resell the newspapers to another set of people; this would take time to arrange, and would obviously be extremely in-convenient. To replace these complicated resales by a simple handing-on of tickets—for that is really what it amounts to—saves an immense amount of trouble. The people who sell clothes to the printers do not take payment for them in news-papers, but in tickets—that is, money. If they like, they can spend some of the money on newspapers, but if they prefer to spend it on bread and cheese, there is nothing to stop them. If they pass on the money to makers of bread and cheese, these people can spend it on newspapers, or they can hand it on to someone else to spend on newspapers, or it can be handed on again. The use of money enables indirect or round-about exchanges to take place, without the goods which are exchanged having to be passed on unnecessarily from one person to another. That is the advantage we get from the use of money; it increases the flexibility of the system of exchanges to an extraordinary extent. But it does not make much difference to the essence of the system. Instead of newspapers being exchanged for clothes directly, the exchange takes place in two stages—the newspapers are sold for money, the money is spent on clothes. And so long as the money is only acquired to be disposed of again without abnormal delay, the division into the two stages proceeds quite smoothly. But sometimes the second stage of the exchange is unduly delayed; goods are sold for money, and yet the money is not spent again until a considerable time has elapsed. When this happens on an unusual scale, the result may be that the system of exchanges gets clogged. The world has had some bad experiences of this sort during the last twenty years; the economic system has shown itself capable of developing monetary diseases of several different kinds. The Theory of Money, which is a special department of economics, is particularly concerned with studying these diseases. Most of it lies outside the field which we shall study in the present volume. But it is impossible to study economic problems at all realistically without paying some attention to these matters, so that we shall be bound to encounter some aspects of these monetary diseases even here.

(ii) *Private Property.* Another complication comes from the ownership of property. Most useful goods cannot be produced by human effort alone; the workers need tools to work with and materials to work on. The products of agriculture are produced from the land. The products of mechanical industry are produced with machines. If agricultural land and industrial plant are in private ownership, the owners of these useful resources may be able to exact a price for their use. That is to say, people may acquire tickets which entitle them to purchase other people's products, not by contributing their labor to the productive process, but by allowing the use of their property. This is a matter of the most profound social significance, since some of the deepest divisions in society turn on the distinction between capitalist and worker. As we go on, we shall find that economics has to concern itself with these divisions to a very considerable extent. All the same, our double description of the economic system does not appear to be affected by the private ownership of property. The owner of property contributes to the productive process by allowing the use of his property in production; to that extent he has to be reckoned as a producer. He exchanges the use of his property for a share in the products of industry and in this way enters into the system of exchanges. It is quite true that he gets these advantages much more easily than the worker does. Or if (as is usually the case) he is also a worker, he gets larger advantages than other workers do from the performance of similar work. If we decide, on the ground of convenience, to reckon the owner of property as producer, we must not allow ourselves, in consequence of this decision, to beg any questions about the desirability of private property as an institution. The institution of private property has to be tried by more searching tests. But we shall find it easier to apply those tests if we begin by getting a clear idea about the working of the system in which private property functions.

(iii) *Government*. The only real qualification to the rule that the economic system can be looked on as a system of exchanges comes from the economic activities of governments, national and local. Some part of the money which people receive, in return for the labor they have performed, or for the property they have allowed to be used, is taken away from them by public authorities in taxes, social security contributions, and the like. In order to see how these taxes fit into the system, we must consider the purposes for which they are raised. Governments sometimes raise taxes in order to make presents to some of their own citizens or to foreigners; under this heading would come such things as tribute to a foreign power, pensions to the ex-soldiers of past wars, relief to the unemployed. All these things are just compulsory gifts from one set of persons to another. Some of them are very sensible and desirable, some very undesirable. But some of the taxes which are raised by governments are raised for another purpose—in order to pay for the employment of people to do work for the good of the community in general, as for example soldiers or policemen or highway maintenance workers. These people's work is part of the Productive Process; but it does not result in the production of such things as can be bought by individual consumers, though consumers in general do undoubtedly desire that they should be provided. The wants which are satisfied by work of this sort are social wants, not individual wants. During wartime a very large proportion of a nation's productive power is turned over to the satisfaction of social wants, for the whole of the armed forces and of the munition industries must be reckoned as working to that end. Even in time of peace, the number of people whose work has to be reckoned as being directed to the satisfaction of social wants is usually quite considerable.

It might be supposed, at first sight, that the proportion of its population working for the satisfaction of social wants would be a measure of the degree of socialization reached by a particular nation. But that is not so. Even in a completely socialized state, like Communist Russia, where the government is very nearly the only employer of labor, the proportion of persons working to satisfy social wants need not be abnormally high. For in a socialist state, the government does not only control the production of those things which are wanted socially, it also controls the production of things wanted individually. (There are, of course, little bits of socialism in this sense even in non-socialist countries—nationalized railways, municipal gasworks, and so on.) In a socialist state, people work for the government, whether they are producing social goods, like roads and parks and military air-planes, or individual goods, like food and clothing. The roads and military airplanes are paid for by the public out of taxes. But the food and clothing are bought from the government, just as they would be bought from private producers in a community which was not organized in a socialist manner. Over the greater part of the field, the socialist government merely acts as an intermediary, in the same way as the private employer. Thus there is nothing in socialism, as such, to prevent us from regarding the economic system as a system of exchanges. Indeed, most of the economic theory in this volume can be applied to a socialist state, just as much as to one which is based on a system of private enterprise. In either case we can look upon the economic system as a co-operation of producers to satisfy consumers' wants (including social wants); or alternatively (apart from the qualification about taxation) we can look upon it as a system of mutual ex-changes.

II

GOODS AND SERVICES

1. The Definition of Production

As soon as we have understood the double nature of the economic system, as it was explained in the previous chapter, we can see that it will be convenient to shape our further classifications in ways which will fit in with each of the two aspects. Henceforward we shall mean by Production any activity directed to the satisfaction of other people's wants through exchange; we shall use a Producer to mean a person engaging in production in this sense. A person whose wants are satisfied by such production we shall call a Consumer. Previously we have used these terms in a looser manner. From now on we shall try to confine them to these precise senses.

Let us see what we are committed to by these definitions. The words producer and consumer are widely used in ordinary speech and in business. But in practical life they do not need to be used very precisely or uniformly, so that they are often used in senses which do not square with our definitions. Farmers, for instance, are fond of drawing a contrast between their own activities as 'producers' of foodstuffs, and those of the traders or retailers, who merely sell or 'distribute' them. On our definition the retailer is a producer just as much as the farmer. The work done by the retailer is a part of the process of satisfying consumers' wants, just as much as the work of the farmer. Milk on the farm and tobacco at the factory are of little use to anyone except the farmer and manufacturer themselves; milk on the doorstep and tobacco in the

28

shop are provided, more or less, where and when the consumer wants them.

The reason why people have been able to persuade themselves that farmers are producers while retailers are not is of course that the word production, used in other senses than the economic, suggests the making of something material, something you can touch or handle, something you can cart about on a truck or bring home in a paper bag. A very great part of economic production does consist in the making of material goods, but quite a large part does not. The trader and retailer deal with material goods, but they do not make them. Their part is to take goods already made and to make them more useful by supplying them at the places and times at which they are wanted. But there are many sorts of workers who are not concerned with the production of material goods at all; doctors, teachers, civil servants and administrators, passenger transport workers, entertainers, domestic servants—all of these are producers in our sense, though they do not produce material products. They do useful work and are paid for it, consequently they count as producers. The things they produce are useful services, not material goods. It is convenient to say that the things produced by producers and consumed by consumers are of two kinds—material 'goods' and immaterial 'services.'

The performance of such services as these is included in production. But if we are to be faithful to our definition, we may not say that all performance of services for other people counts as production. Production is activity directed to the satisfaction of other people's wants through exchange; thus it is only those services which are paid for that have to be included. The most important kind of services which, on this test, have to be left out are the services performed within the family—the work done by wives for their husbands, by parents in looking after their children, and so on. These services are not to be reckoned as productive, because they are

not paid for. It is of course not very convenient that we have
to exclude this essential work from our definition of production, but there does not seem to be any help for it, if we are
to have the advantage of using words in precise and well-
defined ways.[1] The fact that we have excluded it from our
definition does not absolve us from keeping the fundamental
economic importance of this sort of work very much in our
minds.

2. THE CASE OF IMMATERIAL SERVICES

There was a stage in the development of economic thought
when the inclusion in the definition of production of those
direct services which are paid for was not accepted even by
economists. Adam Smith himself confined the term 'productive labor' to that labor which is devoted to the production of
material goods. In a famous passage,[2] he gave a list of such
occupations as must be reckoned to be 'unproductive.' Beginning with 'menial servants,' he goes on:

> The sovereign, for example, with all the officers both of
> justice and of war who serve under him, the whole army and
> navy, are unproductive laborers . . . In the same class must
> be ranked, some both of the gravest and most important, and
> some of the most frivolous professions; churchmen, lawyers,
> physicians, men of letters of all kinds; players, buffoons, musi-
> cians, opera-singers, opera-dancers, etc.

This looks like the same fallacious, or at least uneconomic,
way of thinking which is common among those who approach
economic affairs from the standpoint of the technical processes of manufacture; it is strange to find it in the most famous of all economists. The manufacturer and the farmer naturally think of production as *making* something. We have seen

[1] A further discussion of this, and of some related subjects, will be
found in Appendix, Note A.
[2] *Wealth of Nations,* Book II, ch. 3. (Vol. I, p. 314 in Cannan's
edition.)

that economics has to have a wider definition. Why did Adam Smith suppose the contrary? It was not because he supposed the distinction between material and immaterial products to have any economic significance; his reason was more subtle. Later economists have not been prepared to allow their definition of production to be influenced by it, but they have had to pay much attention to it in other parts of their economic theory. Adam Smith put it in this way:

The labor of the menial servant does not fix or realize itself in any particular subject or vendible commodity. His services generally perish in the very instant of their performance . . . Like the declamation of the actor, the harangue of the orator, or the tune of the musician, the work of all of them perishes in the very instant of its production.

The reason why Smith adopted his odd definition of production was because he was impressed by the fact that the production of most goods takes time, often a very long time, and the consumption of these goods comes afterwards. The significant thing about direct services is that the acts of performing the labor and of enjoying the results of the labor are contemporaneous and inseparable. Goods, on the other hand, have to be produced first and consumed afterwards. The production and consumption of goods form a process. The further classifications, which will concern us in the rest of this chapter and in the next, are all concerned with the economic system considered as a process.

3. The Time Taken in Production. Consumers' Goods and Producers' Goods

On a certain day (say in the spring of 1939) the reader of this book will probably have eaten a piece of bread for lunch. Behind that piece of bread was a considerable history. A day or two earlier it was baked by a baker, who for his stage in the process of breadmaking used various ingredients, notably flour. Some weeks earlier the flour will have been milled out of wheat, various kinds of wheat being very probably mixed together. This wheat will have been harvested, probably during the year 1938, the precise date depending upon the part of the world from which it came. Some months before the time of harvesting the wheat must have been sown, and before the sowing the land on which it was grown must have been plowed. Taking this simple line of operations, from the plowing of the land to the bread on the table, not much less than a year can have elapsed between the start and the finish. Often it will be a good deal more than a year. But this is by no means the whole of the history behind that piece of bread.

At every stage in the process described—plowing, sowing, harvesting, threshing, milling, baking—power or fuel was needed. The power used for plowing may have been nothing more modern than the traditional horse. If so, that horse had to be fed, its feeding stuffs had to be grown, and the growth of the feeding stuffs extends the production process backwards for another series of months. Or the power may have been provided by a tractor; tractors use oil, so that the getting of the oil and its transport to the farm (another stage involving at least a month or two) have also to be reckoned into the process of production of the bread. The same will hold for the power (of whatever kind) used in harvesting, threshing, and milling, also for the coal or electricity used at the bakery. Of course many of these latter processes will be going on simultaneously, so that they do not lengthen the total time taken by the production. Nevertheless, when we have taken the power into account, the whole period looks more like two years than one.

Even this is not all. The tractor, the threshing-machine, the ships and railways used to transport the grain, the elevator used for storing it, the milling machinery used for making the flour, even the baker's oven—all these had to be made at some

time or other, and the reason why they were made was because they would be useful in the manufacture of bread.
Not of course this single piece of bread, which is far too
humble an article to be able to claim for itself alone such
mighty antecedents; but this piece of bread and millions like
it are the reasons why the tractors and elevators and ovens
and the rest of them were brought into being. All this elaborate equipment was in fact constructed as part of the process
of manufacturing bread.

If at some date, three months or six months or a year before the bread appeared upon the table, we had examined
how the process of producing it was getting on, we should
have found that most of the equipment was already made
and in use, while the raw material of the bread was still in
the form of growing crops, or threshed wheat, or bags of
flour. These things can all be looked upon as stages in the
manufacture of the bread. Whatever stage has been reached,
even if it is only the making of a tractor, or the building of
a railroad tank car to transport the oil to feed the tractor,
something has been done which will prove useful and help
towards the final production of bread. The products which
result from these early stages are useful products, but not
products which are directly useful for satisfying the wants of
consumers. Their use is to be found in their employment in
the further stages, at the end of which a product which is
directly wanted by consumers will emerge. It is convenient
to use the term *goods* to cover the products of these earlier
stages, as well as the final product which the consumer purchases. But the products of the earlier stages are called *producers' goods,* to distinguish them from the *consumers' goods,*
which do satisfy the consumers' wants directly.

In our illustration, the bread is a consumers' good; the
wheat, the flour, the tractor, the ship, the oven (and so on)
are producers' goods. A producers' good may be technically
finished, in the sense that the particular operation needed to

produce it is completed (the wheat has been harvested, or the tractor ready for use). Or it may not be technically finished, but still in process, even so far as its own stage is concerned (the grain may be standing in the field, or the flour mill under construction). In either case it is a producers' good, because further stages are needed before the result of the whole process can pass into the consumers' hands. The consumers' good is the end of the whole process; producers' goods are stages on the road towards it.

4. THE TIME TAKEN IN CONSUMPTION. DURABLE-USE AND SINGLE-USE CONSUMERS' GOODS

The production of any consumers' good one cared to select could be similarly shown to consist of a process, occupying in all quite a considerable time, and involving the production of a number of producers' goods on the way. It has next to be noticed that with some consumers' goods, but only with some, consumption is also a process taking an appreciable time. Consumers' goods can be divided, from this point of view, into two classes.

In the first class we have goods, like the bread of our example (and foodstuffs generally), which are used and used up in a single act. The careful housewife may make a loaf of bread last two or three days, but only by dividing it into slices, and consuming the slices at intervals. Each piece of bread is used up as soon as it is used at all. Other consumers' goods which are of the same type are fuel, tobacco, matches, and writing-paper. I shall call these goods *single-use goods.* From the point of view of the consumer, services are similar in character to the single-use goods; but, as we have noticed, they are different on the production side.

The other goods I shall call *durable-use goods.* Houses, furniture, clothes, radios, bicycles, and automobiles are examples of this second class. Their common characteristic is that they can go on being used for considerable periods. The fact that they have been used on one day does not prevent them from being used again on the next. The lengths of time for which they can go on being used vary of course a good deal. A pencil is probably to be reckoned as a durable-use good, in spite of the fact that it is bound to wear out after a few months of use. At the other extreme are such things as old furniture, which can go on being used almost indefinitely (apart from accidents), so long as it is properly looked after and kept in good repair.

The distinction between single-use goods and durable-use goods must not be confused with another distinction, of very similar character, which is commonly made in books on economics. It has been usual among economists to classify consumers' goods into *durable goods* and *perishable goods;* these classes are similar to ours, but they are not exactly the same. *Durable-use* goods are necessarily *durable,* but not all *single-use* are *perishable.* Raw cotton, for example, is a durable good; it can be stored almost indefinitely, and will not deteriorate seriously, so long as it is not used. But it cannot be used without being used up. Thus it is a single-use good. There are many other single-use goods which have a fair degree of durability; tinned and otherwise preserved foods are instances. The fact that they are capable of being stored is a characteristic with important economic consequences. But, for the present at least, it is not the characteristic we want to emphasize. The main classification of consumers' goods is into the single-use and durable-use varieties.

The goods which are purchased by a particular consumer belong partly to one of these varieties, partly to the other. Most of the single-use goods which are purchased have to go on being purchased, week after week, day after day. To have had a good meal yesterday does not prevent one from wanting another good meal today; to have been warm last night does not prevent one from needing to be warmed again this afternoon. Durable-use goods, on the other hand, go on being useful for long periods after they have been bought. Thus they do not need to be bought continuously, but only when the want for them first appears, or when an old one has broken down or become impossibly shabby. It follows that while the purchase of most sorts of single-use goods will take place at fairly regular intervals, purchases of durable-use goods may be very irregular. This is a matter of considerable importance for the running of the productive process. If all the goods which consumers wanted were single-use goods, it would be comparatively easy to organize the economic system so as to keep it running continuously at the same level of activity. The production of durable-use goods is much harder to stabilize, just because the need to purchase such goods is so much less regular. Nevertheless, durable-use goods are of great importance to the consumer. Although food and warmth, the most urgent necessities, are single-use goods, some durable-use goods are essential at any standard of living, while at a higher standard they provide more solid satisfaction than single-use goods can do. Luxury single-use goods mainly take the form of entertainment; luxury durable-use goods range from good housing and good clothing to books and pictures and musical instruments and garden plants, the typical ingredients of a civilized life. People who buy these things can satisfy their wants for them without buying them so regularly as they would buy food. In consequence it is hard to arrange for their production in ways which may not involve economic disturbances. Very much the most difficult case is that of housing; we shall discuss it in more detail in another connection.[3]

5. A Similar Distinction Among Producers' Goods

A similar distinction between single-use and durable-use varieties can be made for producers' goods. Some producers' goods are used up—though this may only mean that they have

[3] See below, ch. VIII.

passed on to the next stage in their production—as soon as they are used at all. Others can go on being used in the same way for long periods. In the illustration we gave the wheat, the flour, and also the oil and the electricity were single-use goods in this sense; the tractor, the ship and the baker's oven were durable-use goods. Generally speaking, single-use producers' goods are the materials used in industry, though half-finished products ought also to be reckoned as single-use goods at another stage. Durable-use producers' goods are the instruments of production—tools, machinery, industrial plant of all kinds. The production of durable-use producers' goods is perhaps even harder to stabilize than the production of durable-use consumers' goods—for much the same reasons. But we are not yet in a position to deal with such questions.

III

CONSUMPTION AND INVESTMENT

1. THE ANNUAL PERIOD

We have now got a general idea of the productive process; but before we can turn to the facts, and try to make sense of them, we need yet another set of definitions. The processes of production and exchange which we have been describing go on more or less indefinitely; they have gone on since the dawn of history, and will go on as long as the human race exists. Although it is true in one sense that particular processes come to an end every day with the completion and sale of finished consumers' goods, these goods have usually been produced along with many others (the durable-use producers' goods used in making them are for the most part still in existence, and being used again). Thus it is very difficult to find a self-contained process which can ever be said to be really over, just as we have seen that it is very difficult to find a date when it can really be said to begin. The only way in which we can limit our investigations, so as not to have to deal with the whole of human history at once, is to select a particular period of time and to confine our attention to the working of the productive process during that period. Usually (though not always) the period which it is most convenient to take is a year.

The statistics of production which were referred to in the introductory chapter of this book usually refer to annual periods. They must, of course, always refer to some period. There is no point in saying that the number of planes produced is 1000, unless one states the time to which this output refers. An output of 1000 planes, spread over two months, is the same rate of output as 500 planes in one month. All measurements of the quantity of production have to refer to a stated period. If we are to use our definitions so as to square with these measurements, our definitions, too, must refer to a particular period of time.

Let us therefore fix our minds on the working of the productive process during a particular year—say 1939. We must think of the whole stream of time as being spread out before us, like a film which has been unwound. We take our scissors and cut out a particular section of the film. Or we may say that we put a spotlight upon this particular year, leaving everything before it and after it in the dark. What is the effect of this limitation upon the classifications we have given?

2. THE PRODUCTIVE PROCESS DURING THE ANNUAL PERIOD

During the year producers will be turning out services and goods of all kinds, single-use goods, durable-use goods, producers' goods, consumers' goods. Most of the single-use goods will be used up in the course of the year, the consumers' goods in the direct satisfaction of consumers' wants, the producers' goods in the making of consumers' goods. It is fairly evident that single-use producers' goods, produced and used up during the year, ought not to be reckoned as part of the total production or output of the year. If we were to include both the bread and the flour out of which it is made, we should be reckoning the same productive effort twice; if we did this, there would be no reason why we should not include the wheat as well, and even the wheat standing in the field as well as the threshed wheat after it has been harvested. Once we allowed ourselves to reckon in both the single-use consumers' goods and the single-use producers' goods out of which they are made, there would be nothing to stop us from dividing the process of production into a large number of stages and counting what is essentially the same product as

many times as we like. This would make the result of our calculation completely arbitrary. 'Double counting' of this sort
has clearly got to be avoided.

Those single-use producers' goods which are produced and
used up during the year must not be counted as part of the
year's production. But does this mean that all producers'
goods have got to be excluded? At first sight one might suppose so, but that is not the case. For the production we are
concerned with is the production of the year 1939, and some
of the durable producers' goods produced during 1939 will
outlast 1939. We have to pay special attention to the carry-
over from one year to another.

At the beginning of the year (the morning of January 1,
1939) there exists in the community a particular stock of
goods, including some from all our four types, but among
which the durable-use goods are no doubt predominant.
These goods are inherited from the previous year; for the
most part they are the result of production in that and in
earlier years. The durable-use consumers' goods inherited
from the previous year include the houses people are living
in, the furniture they are using, the clothes they are wearing, and so on. The durable-use producers' goods will include
the factories, the machinery standing in the factories, the
railways, ships, trucks, tools, and so on which are available
for use in production during the coming year. The single-use
producers' goods which are inherited will include stocks of
materials waiting to be sold. The single-use consumers' goods
(not so many of these) will include such things as foodstuffs
already in the larder; remembering that the retailer is also a
producer, foodstuffs in the shops ought to be reckoned as producers' goods.

This is the position at the beginning of the year. Then the
wheel of time rolls on, and the wheels of production begin
to turn. The goods in the larder are used up, and replaced by
new goods out of the shops—that is to say, producers' goods

pass into consumers' goods. At the same time, the vacant places in the shops are filled by new producers' goods coming forward—that is to say, the materials existing on January 1st are worked on by labor, with the help of durable-use producers' goods, and turned by degrees into finished products. At the same time, other workers using other durable-use producers' goods are preparing new materials. And other workers are making new durable-use goods. So the process goes on, with a continual stream of new consumers' goods passing into consumption, and new single-use producers' goods poking their heads out of the productive process, only to be tucked in again.

Those producers' goods which are produced during the year, and used up in further production within the year, do not count as part of the year's output. They are taken to be included in the consumers' goods of which they are the materials. If we were allowed to extend our gaze into the indefinite future, we should presumably find all the producers' goods incorporating themselves in consumers' goods in this way; but we are not allowed to look forward indefinitely. The year has an end as well as a beginning; many of the consumers' goods in which the producers' goods of this year will be incorporated belong to future years, not to this year. There will be producers' goods left over at the end of this year, just as there were producers' goods left over to this year from the year before.

There is no reason why the quantity of producers' goods bequeathed to 1940 should be the same as that inherited from 1938. The single-use producers' goods inherited from 1938 will, for the most part, have been used up in the production of 1939; new goods will have been produced to replace them, but these new goods may be greater or less in amount than the goods which have been used up. Some of the durable-use producers' goods inherited from 1938 will also have been used up, or worn out, during 1939; and even those which are not worn out will be a year older in January 1940 than they were in January 1939; this will often mean that they have a year's less 'life' left in them. Against this *wear-and-tear* or *depreciation* of the durable-use goods previously existing, has to be set the production of new durable-use goods; but the wear-and-tear may or may not be completely offset by the new production. If it is not completely offset, the quantity of such goods at the disposal of the community will be less at the end of the year than it was at the beginning; if it is more than offset, the quantity at the end of the year will be greater.[1]

The same process of using-up and replacing will occur with consumers' goods as well. The year 1939 will have inherited from its predecessors certain quantities of consumers' goods (mainly durable-use goods, houses and so on); it will hand on certain quantities to its successors. One of the tests of successful productive activity during the year is to be got by comparing the quantities at the end with those at the beginning.

3. THE FACTORS OF PRODUCTION AND THE SOCIAL OUTPUT

The process of production during the year can therefore be described in summary fashion in the following way. At the beginning of the year, there exists a certain stock of goods (all our four kinds) which we may call the Initial Equipment. During the year the initial equipment is worked upon by labor, and there is produced from it a stream of goods. Some of these goods are producers' goods used up again within the year, so that they do not reckon into the year's output; the goods which are included consist partly of consumers' goods, consumed within the year, partly of new equipment, added to the initial equipment as a result of the year's production. The equipment which exists at the end of the year becomes the initial equipment of the next year; it

[1] For some qualification to this statement, see Appendix, Note C.

equals the Initial Equipment of the first year *plus* the New Equipment which has been added *minus* the Wear-and-tear (and other using-up of equipment) which has taken place within the year. This is the scheme of the productive process which we need to have in our minds.

All the product or output of the year comes from Labor and the Initial Equipment; these are therefore called the Factors of Production. The output of goods consists either of consumers' goods consumed within the year (Consumption) or of New Equipment. We can therefore set out our scheme in the form of a table:

Factors of Production = Labor *plus* Initial Equipment

They yield:

Product (or Output) = Consumption *plus* New Equipment

And for the effect on equipment of the year's production:

Initial Equipment 1940 = Initial Equipment 1939 − Wear-and-tear during 1939 + New Equipment produced in 1939.

The classification set out in this table is of fundamental importance for the whole of that part of economics which we shall study in this book. Everything further we have to say is nothing but elaboration of it and application of it to practical problems. For when theory has reached this point, it does begin to be capable of being applied.

4. COMPLICATIONS—LABOR SERVICES AND USE OF HOUSE-ROOM

Before we can proceed to these applications, it should first be noticed, however, that the table as it stands is not quite complete. In the first place, services have been left out of account, as Adam Smith left them out of account—and for what turns out to be substantially the same reason. Just as we have been learning to do, Adam Smith thought of the productive process as consisting of labor working on initial equipment, and making it grow into consumption goods and new equipment. And services did not fit into the picture properly; consequently he excluded them as 'unproductive.' We have decided not to take that way out, and so we must find some way of fitting services into our picture. We can really do so quite easily, if we include the services produced in the year as part of the consumption of the year, and allow for the possibility that these services may have been produced by labor alone, without making use of initial equipment to any important extent. (Of course—and this is even more true today than it was in Smith's time—services may require the assistance of durable-use goods from the initial equipment if they are to be produced. For instance, passenger transport workers provide direct services, but they use a great deal of equipment in providing these services.) This, then, is one of the adjustments which have to be made.

The other adjustment concerns the durable-use consumers' goods, which are included in the initial equipment, and do in fact form an important part of it. Take, for example, houses. The houses which exist at the beginning of the year do for the most part go on being used during the year; they make themselves useful, very useful indeed. The use of a house is a thing for which people are prepared to pay; a man pays rent for the right to live in a particular house, just as he pays for the goods he (or his wife) purchases in the shops. We reckon the goods purchased in the shops as part of the consumption of the year, and since house-room is purchased by consumers in the same sort of way, it is convenient (even if it means some stretching of terms) to reckon the use of house-room as part of the consumption of the year, and consequently also to reckon it as part of the production or output of the year. Strictly speaking, we ought to do the same for all the durable-use consumers' goods contained in the initial equipment (automobiles, for example). But, largely because houses are very frequently rented by their occupiers, while automobiles are usually bought outright, it is usual (even if it is not very logical) to include in this way only the use of houses.[2] Houses are in any case the most important type of durable-use consumers' goods.

Our revised table may therefore be written as follows:

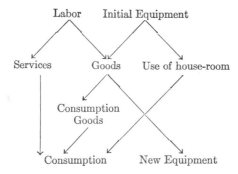

The new houses produced during the year are of course included in the new equipment.

5. DEFINITIONS OF CAPITAL AND INVESTMENT

Our table is now complete, but before we can use it we must introduce two new terms. Instead of our phrase 'initial equipment,' economists usually employ the term 'Capital' (or Wealth); instead of our phrase 'new equipment' the term 'Investment' (or Capital Formation) is now generally used. We had better familiarize ourselves with these important words.

I have so far avoided talking about capital and investment, because these are such outstanding instances of the way in which economists have taken words used by business men and given new meanings to them, meanings which are not (at least on the surface) the same as the business meanings. There is a relation between the meanings of capital and

[2] See Appendix, Note A.

investment in economics and their meanings in business practice; we shall try to get that relation cleared up before we are done. But for the moment it is only the economic meanings which concern us.

In economics, the Capital (or Wealth) of a community consists in the stock of goods of all sorts possessed by the community (either by its individual members, or by associations of its members, such as governments) at a particular moment of time. Thus our 'initial equipment' is the capital possessed by our community on January 1st. In economics, investment is the making of additions to capital. Thus the making of our 'new equipment' is Investment (or Capital Formation).

In this terminology, the Factors of Production are Labor and Capital.[3] The goods and services produced by the factors of production are partly consumed within the year (consumption), partly used to make additions to capital (investment). In order to produce these goods and services, some part of the capital possessed at the beginning of the year is used up (Wear-and-tear or Depreciation of Capital). The net addition to capital within the year is therefore the total production of additions to capital, with depreciation deducted. This net addition to Capital is called Net Investment. Consumption *plus* Net Investment *equals* Net Output.

The definitions given in this last paragraph will become familiar enough as we go on. For the whole program which lies before us is involved in these definitions. In the next two parts of this book we shall study the factors of production—labor and capital. In the last part we shall study the Net Output of the economic system; we shall discuss how it is measured, we shall examine some of the reasons for variations in its size, and we shall examine how it is divided up among different

[3] Land, which nineteenth-century economics used to reckon as a third factor of production, is here included in Capital. For the justification of this arrangement, see below, ch. VIII.

people, so that some are rich and some poor. All these things are developments of the fundamental classifications we have been giving.

Let us then pass on to discuss the factor of production labor. The first problem which has to be considered under that head is the problem of Population. For although not all the people living in a country are producers, it is the total population of the country which mainly governs the number of the workers who are available to take part in the process of production.

PART II

THE FACTORS OF PRODUCTION–LABOR

IV

POPULATION AND ITS HISTORY

1. THE TWO PHASES OF MODERN POPULATION HISTORY

Let us begin by looking at some figures. The following table sets out, in round numbers, the population of a number of countries at various stages in modern history. Since the taking of accurate censuses began in the United States only in 1790, in Great Britain in 1801, and in the other countries at various dates in the nineteenth century, it will be understood that the figures for 1650 are only guesses (though they are careful guesses),[1] while some of the figures even for 1800 and 1850 are not very much better. It is only in the later columns that all the figures are known precisely, but it is not likely that any part of the table is seriously misleading. There have, of course, been some important changes in frontiers during the period; the most important changes have been allowed for.[2]

TABLE I

Population (in millions)

	1650	1800	1850	1900	1940
Great Britain	6	10	21	37	46
France	16	27	35	41	42
Germany	14	20	35	54	70
Italy	13	17	24	32	44
U.S.A.	..	5	23	75	131
Ireland	1	5	6½	4½	4½

[1] They are taken from G. N. Clark, *The Seventeenth Century*, ch. I.
[2] Thus Germany always excludes Austria, France always includes Alsace-Lorraine, Ireland includes Northern Ireland.

When a table of this sort is being examined, it is not the individual figures by themselves which we should study, but the comparison of one figure with another. (This is why it is sufficient to work in round numbers; comparisons can be made more easily if the figures are given approximately; detail would distract the eye, without adding anything of importance.) In the table before us, at least two kinds of comparisons can be made. By looking down the columns, we can compare the populations of different countries at the same dates; the points which then emerge are mainly of political interest, though of very great political interest indeed. The greatness of France under Louis XIV and under Napoleon is reflected in the relatively high population of France in the 1650 and 1800 columns; the strength of Germany and the weight of the United States in the modern world are indicated in the columns for 1900 and 1940. Military strength is not entirely a matter of population, but population is an important element in it.

From the economic point of view, a study of the table by horizontal rows is more instructive. Every one of the countries in the list (with the exception of Ireland—included just because it is an exception) shows increases in population throughout the whole period; usually they show enormous increases. The increase in population which has taken place in Europe and America during the last three centuries is one of the most stupendous facts in history. It is quite probable that no widespread population increase was ever both so rapid and so prolonged. But when we look at the table more closely, it becomes apparent that the increase has not proceeded at all smoothly or regularly; it has been much faster at some times and places than at others. It will be useful to examine these variations in detail.

At first sight, the simplest way of comparing the rates of increase at different stages would seem to be by calculating the percentages by which the various populations increased between 1650 and 1800, 1800 and 1850, and so on. But since the intervals between our dates are of different lengths, these percentages would be less informative than one could wish. It is better to calculate the *average* rate of increase in each of the intervals—that is to say, the annual rate of increase which, if maintained over the whole interval, would have resulted in the actual increase of population which we find. Since the annual rates of increase are of course small (many of them less than 1 per cent), it is more convenient to express them as rates per thousand than as rates per hundred (percentages).[3]

TABLE II

Average Rates of Population Increase (per thousand per annum)

	1650-1800	1800-50	1850-1900	1900-40
Great Britain	3	14	11	5
France	3	5	3	1
Germany	2	11	9	7
Italy	2	7	6	8
U.S.A.	..	31	24	14
Ireland	9	5	−16	−1

The first thing which strikes one when looking at this new table is the extremely rapid rate at which the populations of nearly all the countries were expanding during the interval 1800-1850. Even the French, whose rate of increase has nearly always been slow, increased faster than usual during this half-century. Ireland, which again looks like an exception, is here less of an exception than it looks. The Irish population continued to increase at a rate of 9 per thousand until 1840, but between 1840 and 1850 it started falling, as a result of the Potato Famine. The general impression one gets from the table as a whole is that the history of population during the

[3] In order to calculate the annual rate of increase which would turn a population of 6 millions into one of 10 millions in 150 years, we have to solve the equation: $(1 + x/1000)^{150} = 10/6$. Take logarithms of both sides and it comes out at once. The annual rate of increase must be approximately 3.4 per thousand.

last two centuries has passed through two distinct phases, during the first of which there was a great acceleration in the rate of growth of population, while during the second the brake was put on more or less violently. These are in fact the two phases which have to be explained.

Changes in population come about in two ways: by Natural Increase or Decrease (excess of births over deaths, or vice versa), and by Migration. The figures in our tables are affected by migration to an appreciable extent, but not sufficiently to disturb the general pattern. The population of the United States has been greatly increased by immigration; but the great mass of the nineteenth-century immigrants came in after 1850, so that the astounding rate of growth of American population during the early nineteenth century (31 per thousand per annum) was almost entirely a natural increase. What the immigrants did was to prevent the increase from slowing up as rapidly as it would have done without them. The decline in Irish population after 1840 was largely a result of emigration, but not entirely. The most significant difference which is made to our figures when we allow for migration is in the case of Italy. Emigration from Italy was particularly great during the period 1880-1910; the rate of growth of Italian population shown in the last two columns of our table is therefore less than the natural increase. If one had figures for the Italian population, *whether living in Italy or not,* it is probable that the rates of growth in the successive periods would be something like 2, 7, 8, 11, instead of 2, 7, 6, 8, of our table. The Italian rate of natural increase went on rising far into the twentieth century; it is only in very recent years that signs have begun to appear that Italy also is passing into the second phase.

Let us take the two phases in turn and enquire (1) why the rate of population increase accelerated and (2) why it slowed up.

2. BIRTH RATES AND DEATH RATES

The Natural Increase of Population takes place by an excess of Births over Deaths; consequently the rate of Natural Increase (that is, the rate of growth in Table II adjusted for migration) equals the difference between the Birth Rate (number of births per thousand of population per annum) and the Death Rate (number of deaths per thousand per annum). A high rate of natural increase must be due to a wide gap between the birth rate and the death rate; but the gap may be wide because the birth rate is exceptionally high or because the death rate is exceptionally low. An increase rate of 10 per thousand (which is enough to cause quite a rapid expansion of population) may be due to a birth rate of 35 and a death rate of 25, or to a birth rate of 25 and a death rate of 15. It seems probable (though naturally one cannot say for certain) that the more or less stabilized populations which seem to have been the general rule in the early eighteenth century were due to a combination of high birth rate with high death rate—both of them in the neighborhood of 30 per thousand, with only a narrow gap between them. The principal development which upset this primitive equilibrium was a marked fall in the death rate, due (beyond all doubt) to the improvements in sanitation, diet, and medical skill which were beginning to be effective in the north of Europe by the middle of the eighteenth century, though they failed to exercise any appreciable influence in the more backward countries for some time after 1800.

Birth rates and death rates for England and Wales are set out in Chart I. By 1780 (which is as far back as it is really safe to make estimates) the English death rate was already falling quite steeply; there is good reason to suppose that the fall began some years before that. It continued until about 1820; after that it was checked for some time (this is where the bad sanitary conditions in the new industrial towns seem to come in), but it was resumed after 1870. As a result of the whole process the death rate has been reduced from nearly 30 per thousand in 1780 to about 12 per thousand in the 1930's.

As many Americans needing birth certificates have lately learned to their sorrow, reasonably full records of births and

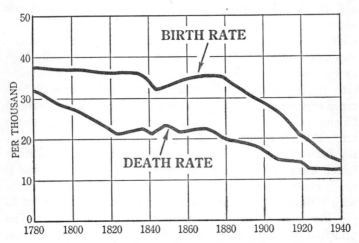

CHART I. BIRTH AND DEATH RATES IN ENGLAND AND WALES, 1780-1940

deaths have not been kept in all parts of the country until very recently. The 'registration area' for which the Bureau of the Census calculates death rates came to include the entire country only in 1933; and for long-term comparisons we are pretty well restricted to a period of 40 years and to the 'registration states as of 1900,' covering about 40 per cent of population.[4] For this area the death rate fell from an average of

[4] The defects of our knowledge, of course, do not spring from the *size* of the sample; a 40 per cent sample is not perceptibly less reliable statistically than a 90 per cent sample for a population the size of the United States, if both samples are selected on the same principles. The difficulty with death rates is the *composition* of the sample, which con-

15.8 per thousand in 1901-5 to 11.5 in 1930. This down-trend, which still continues, reflects largely a prodigious fall in the number of deaths per thousand among children less than 5 years old; but for older children and adults up to age 45, death rates have also fallen by from 30 per cent to 60 per cent of the 1901-5 averages. Mortality among persons over 45, however, is almost as great per thousand as at the beginning of the century.

During the period for which we have reliable statistics for the United States, the birth rate has been far below the level of over 35 per thousand—which must have existed in the early nineteenth century—and has been falling rapidly. From 25 per thousand in 1915, the birth rate dropped below 20 at the end of the 1920's, and was below 17 in the late 1930's. From 11 per thousand in 1915, the excess of births over deaths dropped to about 5 in the late 1930's.

The rise in the rate of population growth (our first phase) was mainly due to a fall in the death rate; the slowing-up in the second phase is undoubtedly due to a fall (a much more sudden fall) in the birth rate. As appears from the chart, the English birth rate turned definitely downwards about 1870; in sixty years it fell from 35 per thousand to 15. The German birth rate did not leave the 35 level until after 1900, but it fell very precipitously when it did decline. During the 1930's it has been usually a little below 20, the lowest point (15) having been touched at the time of the social and economic collapse in 1932. The Italian birth rate has been falling since 1922. The tendency to a falling birth rate is very widespread in the world we now live in; it is one of the major economic facts of the twentieth century.

sists almost entirely of densely populated eastern states with above-average death rates.

3. The Decline in the Birth Rate

What are the causes of this fall in the birth rate? In spite of all the work which has been done on the subject, we do not altogether know. The explanation most commonly given is the practice of birth control, or contraception. But although the improvement of methods of birth control may explain how people *can* limit their families without undue difficulty, it does not explain why they should *want* to limit their families so very drastically. (Furthermore, it would appear that in several of the continental countries where the same fall in the birth rate has taken place, the method most frequently used is not contraception but abortion; abortion is a repulsive method, often dangerous to health and ordinarily illegal, so that the desire for family limitation must be very strong indeed for people to adopt it.) What has to be explained is the motive or motives which have led to so general a recourse to family limitation; naturally that is not a thing which can easily be discovered.

It is possible, however, that some light may be thrown on the matter if we look back at the period before 1870, when contraception is not likely to have been of much importance, and when nevertheless we do find considerable variations in birth rates. As appears from our chart, the birth rate in England was running at 35 or over during the whole period from 1780 to 1870 (except for an appreciable dip in the 1840's). This is a distinctly high rate, but even higher rates have occurred in North America, some as high as 50 per thousand. In France, on the other hand, the birth rate ran at not much over 25 during the greater part of the nineteenth century. These variations are quite sufficient to make a large difference to the rate of population expansion; how are they to be explained?

The explanation which is usually given for the relatively

low birth rate in nineteenth-century France is to connect it with the system of landholding. A settled peasant population, owning its own farms, has a strong incentive to restrict the size of the family. Openings outside agriculture are limited; younger children can only be provided for by dividing the family holding—that is to say, at the expense of the elder. Consider the contrast between this situation and that in the New World. American population could increase as rapidly as it did between 1800 and 1840 because parents needed to feel no responsibility for providing careers for their children; the career provided itself—'out West.' There was nothing to stop population from expanding at a fabulous pace.

Something of the same unlimited opportunity was provided in a more sordid way by the Industrial Revolution in England. Children became wage-earners at an early age; it cost parents very little trouble to ensure that their children had as good prospects of life as the parents had had themselves—though these prospects were often poor enough in all conscience. But as the standard of living (and in particular the standards of education) improved, the responsibilities of bringing up a family increased very markedly. The first dip in the English birth rate is suspiciously contemporaneous with the early factory acts, which limited the employment of children in industry. The later, and more permanent, decline follows upon the introduction of compulsory education. We cannot prove a connection, but it would not be surprising if the additional burden on the parents, due to their having to support their children up to the age of 14, without getting much in exchange even in the way of help about the home, had a good deal to do with the decline in the birth rate. Elementary education may be free in itself; but children cannot take advantage even of elementary education, unless they are properly brought up by their parents; it costs money (with the improvement in standards, it costs more than it did) to bring them up properly.

The reasons for the fall in the birth rate still have a good deal of mystery about them, but this is at least one possible explanation. It is not an ignoble explanation; it means that the quantity of the population has been endangered in the process of improving its quality.[5] That is a kind of thing which is very liable to happen in human affairs, especially economic affairs; progress on one front is accompanied by retrogression on another. This does not mean that all real progress is ultimately impossible; the line can usually be straightened out later on. In this case the line will certainly have to be straightened out, for the fall in the birth rate has reached a point where it has become a social problem of the first magnitude. It is already possible to foresee some of the difficulties in which it is certain to involve us.

4. THE FUTURE OF POPULATION

It is more possible to make reasonably accurate prognostications about the future in matters of population than it is in most human affairs. This is because of the simple fact that all those people who will be over 20 years of age in twenty years' time are alive now; thus (apart from immigration) we can set an upper limit to the adult population of any country twenty years hence with complete confidence. On the basis of this known fact a good deal more about that future population can be guessed, and guessed with some assurance. Thus we cannot tell how many babies will be born during the next twenty years; but we do know almost exactly how many females, now living, are due to pass through the child-bearing

[5] A supplementary explanation is the improvement in employment opportunities for women. This reduces the percentage of women who marry, raises the age of marriage for those who do marry, and postpones having children after marriage to permit the young wife to continue at work.

age during the next twenty years—and that has a great deal to do with the number of births.

In order to estimate the future population of a country, we do not merely continue the birth-rate and death-rate curves in the same directions as they have been proceeding in the recent past (Chart I), and observe that they will intersect. We can do a great deal better than that, for we have additional information in the age-distribution of the present population, and in records for mortality at different ages.

The population of any country at any date can be divided into age-groups, so many ten-year-olds, so many eleven-year-olds, and so on. In a completely stationary population, where the same number of births had taken place every year for the previous seventy years, these age-groups would form a descending series, with rather fewer persons in each age-group than in the one before it (because a certain number of people die at every age). A typical age-distribution for a stationary population of this sort is shown in Chart II (B).

In this diagram, resembling a Christmas tree, the branches on the left-hand side of the trunk represent male population, those on the right-hand side female population. Ages are measured from the bottom upward. The length of each branch shows the percentage of males or females at the age in question.

If now this population began to increase by extra births, the new generations coming into the junior age-groups would be larger than the older generations were when they came in; consequently, the Christmas tree would begin to swell at the bottom, the lower branches growing relatively to the others. As time went on, this swelling would travel upwards; but if the number of births went on increasing, the numbers in the lower age groups would still be disproportionately high relatively to those in the higher age-groups. The slope of the tree would be distinctly flattened as compared with the stationary case.

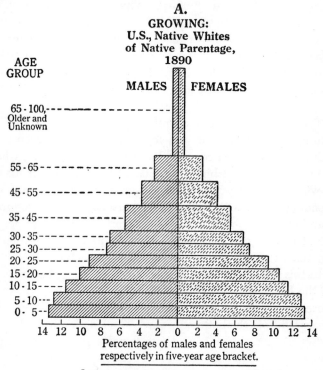

A.
GROWING:
U.S., Native Whites
of Native Parentage,
1890

Large proportion in low age groups reflects large and growing number of births.

SOURCE: U.S. Census

CHART II. AGE DISTRIBUTIONS IN GROWING AND STABLE POPULATIONS AND IN POPULATION ON VERGE OF DECLINE

Chart II (A) represents a rapidly growing population—the population of Americans of native parentage [6] in 1890. The rapid shortening of the branches as the eye glances up the

[6] This is shown rather than the whole population because of the disturbing effects of immigration on the age distribution. By 1970, however,

tree reflects partly the relatively high mortality of the middle nineteenth century. But chiefly it reflects the fact that there

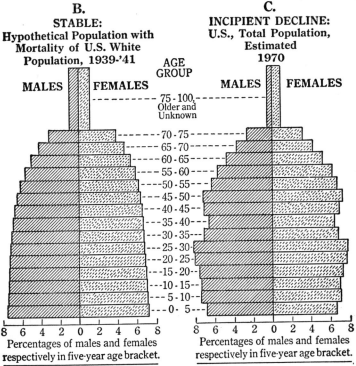

B.
STABLE:
Hypothetical Population with Mortality of U.S. White Population, 1939-'41

C.
INCIPIENT DECLINE:
U.S., Total Population, Estimated 1970

AGE GROUP

MALES   FEMALES   MALES   FEMALES

75 - 100, Older and Unknown

70 - 75
65 - 70
60 - 65
55 - 60
50 - 55
45 - 50
40 - 45
35 - 40
30 - 35
25 - 30
20 - 25
15 - 20
10 - 15
5 - 10
0 - 5

8   6   4   2   0   2   4   6   8   8   6   4   2   0   2   4   6   8

Percentages of males and females respectively in five-year age bracket.

Percentages of males and females respectively in five-year age bracket.

Shrinkage from one age-group to next reflects mortality only. Large proportion in old age.

Previous growth shown by sharp tapering at top; declining number of births by tapering at bottom.

SOURCE: U.S. Census

were more births in 1880-90 than in 1870-80, more in 1870-80 than in 1860-70, etc.

The prospective age distribution of the United States population for 1970, as estimated by the National Resources Plan-

the period of heavy immigration will be so remote as to make this disturbance much less serious.

ning Board, is shown in Chart II (C). The part of the diagram representing people over age 30 represents survivors from among those already living when the estimate was made. The sharp tapering at the top reflects partly expected mortality,[7] partly the effect of the fact that the momentum of nineteenth-century population growth continued to increase the number of births up to the early 1920's. The tapering halfway down the tree reflects the shrinkage in the absolute number of births which began in 1924.

The bulge just below age 30 (representing people born in 1940-45) registers the sharp rise of the early war years in births—the consequence partly of prosperity, partly of wartime social conditions, and partly of the fact that the record number of people who were born 20 years earlier were just reaching the age of marriage. The renewed decline in the number of births to be expected after 1945 explains the tapering at the bottom of the diagram.

These estimates show that unless the size of the American family increases a good deal we shall undergo a population decline. Paradoxically, however, it will probably not be until after 1980 or even 1990 that this decline will appear in the figures of total population. The reason for the paradox is that a population in the first stages of decline has a larger proportion of people in the ages from 20 to 45 [8] than either a rapidly growing or a stable population, as may be seen by comparing the three trees of Chart II. People in these ages are the people who have children, so that the bulge in these age-groups tends to slow down the fall in the birth rate. On

[7] War losses, which were not allowed for, will further reduce the male population aged (in 1970) 45 to 60. The estimates are based on assumptions of 'medium fertility, medium mortality, and no immigration.'

[8] On the female side, 34.4 per cent of the population represented by Chart II (A), 34.0 per cent of the population represented by Chart II (B), and 35.7 per cent of the population represented by Chart II (C) are aged 20-45.

the other hand, people in these ages do not die off very fast.[9] Thus the presence in our population of large numbers of young adults keeps the population from shrinking in total numbers long after the number of births has fallen below the level required to maintain population in the long run.

Population decline is inevitable under the 'small family system' to which we are at present adjusted. If the normal family has two children, which seems to be the present standard, there are no extra children to replace those who fail to marry or whose marriages are childless. In order to prevent the population from falling, families of three or four children must be quite common—and that is hardly likely to happen unless families of five and six cease to be the extreme rarities they are today.

Whenever the normal number of children is sufficiently increased, the forces working toward population decline can be checked. But just as the momentum of population increase is enough to carry the total population figure upward for a few decades after births come to be too low for replacement, the momentum of a population decline once started may be considerable. Unless the upturn in the size of family comes soon, the date at which the population can be stabilized may be fifty years or more in the future, and the level at which it can be stabilized may be a good deal below the present population.

Would this be a bad thing? We will hold over that question to the next chapter.

[9] In 1940, the death rates per thousand in the different age groups ranged as follows:

Age	25-34	35-44	45-54	55-64	65-74	75-84	Over 85	All ages, including children
Rate	3.1	5.2	10.6	22.3	48.0	112.6	228.9	10.8

In a stable population with the same death rates in each age group, Chart II (B), the large proportion in the high age groups would raise the over-all death rate by about 5 per thousand.

V

THE ECONOMICS OF POPULATION

1. DANGERS IN EACH DIRECTION

There have been two episodes in the development of economic thought when economists have devoted a particular amount of their attention to the problem of population. One was at the beginning of the nineteenth century, when (as we have seen) the growth of population was proceeding at such an exceptionally rapid rate; the other has been quite recently, when the populations of most countries have finished, or nearly finished, their upward surge, and we are having to expect a future decline. It is not surprising that T. R. Malthus, with whose *Essay on Population* (1798) serious discussion of the population problem really begins, should have been profoundly troubled by the perils of population becoming too large, through a rise in numbers proceeding unchecked; nor that his successors at the present day should be more inclined to emphasize the opposite danger, of population becoming too small, or getting smaller. The change in emphasis is a natural result of the events described in the last chapter.

It is indeed generally accepted that there are dangers in each direction. Long before systematic economic thought began to develop these dangers were noted: 'the one part through the small number of inhabitants becometh desolate, and the other being overcharged, oppressed with poverty.' [1] The dangers of underpopulation (too small a population for economic efficiency) and of overpopulation (too large a popu-

[1] Machiavelli, *History of Florence* (in Tudor Translations series, p. 70).

66

lation) are both real dangers, though they arise from different causes. The studies which have been made in the subject, both in the time of Malthus and in our own day, have enabled us to appreciate these dangers much more precisely.

2. Underpopulation and Small-Scale Production

To begin with the case of underpopulation. It is easy to appreciate how it is possible for a country to be underpopulated if one considers the case of a small colony, with few people, and poor communications. Such a colony, obliged to satisfy its own wants by its own labor, would hardly fail to be miserably poor; for the organization of its economic system would be inevitably rudimentary and unproductive. It would be hampered by fewness of numbers in two different ways. In the first place, there might be things which would badly need doing, but could not possibly be done by a small number of workers. Such things as the building of bridges over large rivers would be physically impossible. The building of a railway between two distant places might not be impossible physically, but would be impossible practically, because it would take so long that the makers could hardly hope to live to see the fruit of their labors. But a much more important disadvantage would be the limit imposed upon specialization. The high efficiency of modern industry comes about very largely as a result of specialization; workers are specialized to particular jobs, and as a result they acquire great dexterity at those jobs; their efficiency is further increased by their use of highly specialized equipment. Very little of this specialization would be possible in a small colony with a few thousand inhabitants. It would be useless for people to specialize themselves on the sort of operations needed to produce automobiles on a large scale, if the maximum number of cars which could be sold in a year was a few dozen. With so limited a market for their products, the automobile manufacturers would spend most of their time standing idle, with the result that they would actually use their time more productively if they spent it in tilling the soil. But for the same reason the methods of cultivation used would have to be of a primitive character; modern agriculture, with its use of machinery and fertilizers, is itself dependent upon large-scale industry; tractors and binders could not be produced if only a few could be sold in a year. The same would be the case for nearly every specialized occupation one could think of; a small isolated community could only produce in unspecialized and consequently primitive ways. In the technical language of economic theory, it would be unable to take advantage of the *economies of large-scale production.*

These disadvantages of underpopulation are in fact experienced even today by small communities in out-of-the-way places, though they are greatly moderated by the opportunity of trading with the outside world. Trading enables the small community to specialize in suitable lines, even though it may be unable to sell at home all it produces in these lines; for it can sell its surpluses abroad, receiving in exchange for them things which it would have been unable to produce at home, or (and this is even more important) larger quantities of things which it could have produced at home in smaller quantities if it had not sought for the advantages of employing its labor in specialized ways. Sometimes the disadvantages of a small population can be completely overcome by this means; but the cost of transporting goods to and from distant countries is sometimes too great for it to be possible to carry specialization through foreign trading very far. The costs of transporting goods from one area to another are often artificially increased by the protective policies of governments. It was for this reason that many of the small states with which Europe was littered after the Peace of Versailles were made poor by the smallness of their populations; they paid with poverty for what proved to be a very transitory independence.

3. OVERPOPULATION AND SHORTAGE OF LAND

The dangers of overpopulation spring from a different source. As we have seen, the greater part of production takes place by the combination of labor with capital equipment. If population increases, the factor of production labor becomes more plentiful; and this will usually enable the total amount of goods and services produced to be increased. But the increase in population also involves an increase in the wants which have to be satisfied; the extra workers have to be fed and clothed and housed, so that unless the increase in production is proportional to the increase in population, the average standard of living will fall. (That is to say, if population increases by 2 per cent, the people will be poorer *on the average,* unless total production increases by at least 2 per cent at the same time. If production increases by less than 2 per cent, the *average productivity* of the workers is diminished by the increase in their numbers.)

It is probable that an increase in population will be attended by a fall in average productivity, if the increase in the factor of production labor is not accompanied by an increase in the factor of production capital. For if this happens, the same amount of capital equipment will have to be shared out amongst a larger number of workers; each of them, therefore, will have on the average a smaller amount of equipment to work with. Sharing specialized equipment is of course a very awkward business; it is probable that in the first instance many of the extra workers could only be taken on as 'helpers.' At a later stage, when equipment wears out and comes to be replaced, it may be possible to replace it in forms which make better use of the extra labor. But so long as it is a matter of squeezing the extra workers into a productive system which is not really any better provided with equipment, the amount of goods produced is not likely to increase in the same proportion as the labor force has increased—excepting in cases when the larger supply of labor enables new economies of exceptional importance to be derived from specialization.

This is in principle the way in which the danger of over-population arises; as population increases, its average productivity may fall, because of the lack of a similar expansion in capital equipment. Overpopulation will arise only if capital equipment fails to expand sufficiently. Quite apart from the question of specialization, it is often possible to overcome the shortage of equipment by increasing the supply. If this can be done, the danger of overpopulation disappears.

There is, however, one particular sort of capital equipment which is not capable of being increased by human agency to any appreciable extent; it is agricultural land.[2] A community which runs short of land can sometimes overcome the shortage by seizing land from its neighbors; apart from military action of that sort, very little can be done to remedy a shortage of land, though up to a point the evil can be moderated by using the land more economically, or by making improvements in its quality. So long as a country's population remains small, relatively to the size of its territory, there is not likely to be any shortage of land; there may be land of good quality which remains uncultivated. The danger of overpopulation arises when the best land is already being intensively cultivated, so that extra food for extra mouths can only be secured by scratching at stony soils, or pushing the boundary of cultivation higher and higher up mountain slopes. The reality of such overpopulation (at least within certain localities) will be appreciated by anyone who has visited Puerto Rico, or seen the congested districts of western Ireland, or watched the Italian peasant cultivating a little pocket of ground perched among cliffs in his congested area near Naples. India and

[2] It was for this reason that nineteenth-century economists used to reckon land as a third factor of production, alongside labor and capital, instead of regarding it as a particular kind of capital equipment, which is what we have decided to do.

China contain between them one half of the human race; large parts of their peoples are living in abject poverty, because immense populations are concentrated in small areas, and have to feed themselves from those areas. Overpopulation through shortage of land is one of the great causes of the poverty there is in the world.

4. Means of Overcoming the Shortage of Land

In the light of this terrible possibility, the overpopulation scare of the early nineteenth century becomes readily intelligible. The British population was increasing at an alarming rate, doubling itself in half a century; how (asked Malthus and his followers) would it be possible to feed so vast a population from the limited area of the island? At that time little assistance was got from imports; the shortage of land was a real nightmare. There seemed to be no way of avoiding a future in which all the luxuries and conveniences of life would have to be sacrificed to the dire necessity of getting bread; and when at last even bread might be lacking. If the rise in population continued, that was the fate which appeared to be in store sooner or later.

As we know, this fate has been avoided. The British population is now more than four times what it was in 1800, yet (excepting in war time) it is in no danger of suffering seriously from want of food. But the fact that the fears of the Malthusians were not realized does not mean that they were idle. Malthus had discerned a real peril; England avoided it, but it was not avoided in another case closely parallel to England's—in the case of Ireland.

At the time when Malthus was writing, the Irish population was half the size of the English, and it was growing at much the same rate. But in the Irish case, the growth of population began to be checked after 1820, and checked by shortage of food. Ireland experienced a series of famines, which culminated in the great famine of 1846. Today the Irish population is only about one-tenth of the size of the English.

How was it that England avoided the danger to which Ireland succumbed? If England had been obliged to support her population entirely from her own soil, there can be little doubt that England would have experienced a similar disaster before the nineteenth century was over. In fact, in the years before improvements in ocean transport made it easy to import foodstuffs on a great scale, food in England was very scarce; the Corn Law agitation was the sign of a real scarcity, the premonitory symptom of what might have grown into a much greater calamity. As it was, the cheapening of transport made it possible for the English people to draw upon the ample supplies of agricultural land in the New Worlds of America and Australia, and so to remedy their own shortage. But how was it possible for the English people to save themselves in this way, and not possible for the Irish to do so as well?

The reason is that imports have to be paid for. If the agricultural land available in England was becoming small relatively to the population, England possessed other natural resources, in the form of coal and other minerals, which were absent in Ireland, and she was continually adding to her manmade equipment, her factories and mines, her ships and her railways. All these resources enabled her to produce plenty of goods which she could exchange against foodstuffs from overseas. Although she was short of agricultural land, her capital equipment as a whole was continually increasing. The things which she could produce with this equipment were most of them unsuitable for satisfying the basic need for food, but that difficulty could be removed by trading with other countries. Even so, of course she would have been unable to remove it so easily if her general productive power had not been increasing at such a rapid pace.

5. How Far Such Means Are Likely to Be Available

When the matter is looked at in this way, it suggests a conclusion of very wide significance. As the problem appeared to the Malthusians, shortage of agricultural land was an insuperable obstacle; when once the population of any country had reached the point where shortage of land becomes acute, the people would be bound to suffer from poverty, poverty which could only be remedied by the population becoming smaller.[3] Today, as a result of the improvements in transport which have taken place, the position of overpopulated countries has become, potentially at least, much less desperate. Although the peoples of particular countries and particular regions do suffer from a shortage of agricultural land, the human race as a whole does not suffer in that way to any serious extent. And so long as there is plenty of agricultural land in the world as a whole, overpopulation of particular areas can usually be remedied by industrialization. It does indeed sometimes happen that large populations are concentrated in regions which are very unsuitable for industrialization, owing to poorness of natural resources (not agricultural only) or bad communications; but for the most part overpopulation can be remedied by an increase in the amount of capital equipment—in those kinds of equipment which can be increased by human effort. That is just what industrialization implies.

However, as we have seen in our description of the productive process,[4] the way by which capital equipment is increased is by the use of some part of the community's productive power during a period for the construction of new equipment (investment). Productive power can be used for

[3] A favorite modern version of this Malthusian argument is discussed in Appendix, Note B.
[4] Ch. III, above.

the production either of consumption goods or of investment goods. Now when the average productivity of a community is low, it will have the greatest difficulty in producing enough consumption goods to satisfy the basic necessities of life; so it will have little productive power to spare for the production of investment goods. Countries which are in this position are involved in a vicious circle. Only a larger supply of capital equipment would enable them to escape from the toils to be able to produce that equipment for themselves. Thus they cannot escape without assistance from outside. What means there are of giving them that assistance we shall consider later.[5]

Once a country has become sufficiently wealthy to be able to increase its capital equipment from its own resources at a rapid rate, the danger of overpopulation will usually be remote. This is the position in which most 'advanced' countries have usually found themselves in the twentieth century. Once this stage has been reached, the balance of economic advantage may well be on the side of an increasing population. Quite apart from the economies of large-scale production, the increase in population affords a stimulus to investment; new houses have to be produced for the extra people to live in, new machines to make clothes and other conveniences for them, and so on. A considerable part of the labor force in such progressive countries will be specialized on the production of such investment goods. This means (paradoxically enough) that it is actually easier to maintain employment (prevent unemployment) when population is increasing. It is not impossible that slowing-up of population increase may have been one of the things responsible for the exceptional unemployment which occurred during the 1930's. The approaching decline in population is undoubtedly going to set

[5] See below, ch. XII, paragraph 5.

an awkward problem of reorganization to the countries which are affected by it—not necessarily an insuperable problem, but a decidedly delicate one. Declining population may actually involve us in greater difficulties on the side of production than would arise from further increase.

VI

THE SPECIALIZATION OF LABOR

1. POPULATION AND LABOR FORCE

Population is only the first of the economic problems connected with labor as a factor of production. The contribution of labor to the productive process depends in the first place on the number of workers, secondly on the kinds of work they can do, and thirdly on the effort they put into their work. This chapter will consider mainly the second of these questions; the third will be taken up in the chapter which follows it.

We must begin, however, by winding up the argument about numbers. The number of persons who work and earn their living in a particular country is always far less than the total population. This is by no means a matter of mere idleness; it is mostly because non-workers are below working age, or incapacitated, or have other things to do. Thus at the census of 1940 the population of the United States was classified as in Tables IIIA and IIIB.

Among the 'non-workers,' as may be seen from Table IIIB, the most numerous group are the housewives. Needless to say, housewives are among the least idle people in a community. But both the census concept of labor force and our concept of production compel their omission. Students are the other major group of non-workers who are active; the other groups consist largely of persons past working age or incapacitated by injury or disease.

Within the labor force there is always a reserve of unemployed—those seeking work or holding government emergency

TABLE IIIA

Population and Working Force in the United States, 1940

| | Number (millions) | | | Per cent of all persons aged 14 and over | | |
	Total	Male	Female	Total	Male	Female
Total population	131.7	66.1	65.7			
Persons under 14	30.6	15.5	15.1			
Persons over 14: potential working force	101.1	50.6	50.5	100.0	100.0	100.0
In labor force	52.8	39.9	12.8	52.2	79.0	25.4
Not in labor force	48.3	10.6	37.7	47.8	21.0	74.6

TABLE IIIB

Composition of 'Non-Working' Group in the United States, 1940

| | Number (millions) | | | Per cent of all persons aged 14 and over | | |
	Total	Male	Female	Total	Male	Female
Persons doing own housework	28.9	0.33	28.7	28.6	0.5	56.7
Students	9.0	4.6	4.4	8.9	9.1	8.7
Persons unable to work	5.3	3.0	2.3	5.2	5.9	4.6
Persons in institutions	1.2	0.8	0.4	1.2	1.5	0.8
Others, and not reported	3.9	2.0	1.9	3.9	4.0	3.8
Total non-workers	48.3	10.6	37.7	47.8	21.0	74.6

jobs. In the best of times, there is always some unemployment of 'frictional' or 'seasonal' character—people who are in process of changing jobs, or waiting through a slack season till their usual jobs reopen. Even under war stress, it is hard to get unemployment in the United States below one million. In ordinarily prosperous years, such as 1939 and 1940, unemployment has often been several times this minimum figure; and in years of acute depression like 1932 and 1933 it has been several times greater again. The unemployed shade off in one direction into persons who are not in the labor force, in the other into persons who have jobs but are momentarily not working because of temporary lay-offs, illness, etc. The employment situation of the labor force in 1940 is shown in Table IIIC.

TABLE IIIC

Employment Status of Labor Force in the United States, 1940

	Number (millions)			Per cent of all persons aged 14 and over		
	Total	Male	Female	Total	Male	Female
Employed and at work	44.0	33.2	10.8	43.6	65.7	21.4
Having jobs, but not momentarily at work	1.1	0.8	0.3	1.1	1.6	0.6
Total having jobs	45.2	34.0	11.1	44.7	67.3	22.0
On relief work (W.P.A., etc.)	2.5	2.1	0.5	2.5	4.1	0.9
Seeking work: Experienced workers	4.3	3.4	0.9	4.3	6.7	1.9
New workers	0.8	0.5	0.3	0.8	0.9	0.6
Without jobs	7.6	5.9	1.7	7.6	11.7	3.4
Total labor force	52.8	39.9	12.8	52.2	79.0	25.4

In times either of acute unemployment or of wartime stress the labor force expands at the expense of the non-worker group. When a man is out of work for some time, his wife and perhaps his children are more likely to look for work than when he has a steady job. In wartime, patriotic incentives, greater willingness of employers to take pains with new or handicapped workers, and other factors bring out millions of persons who ordinarily are not on the labor market. In this book it is not possible to get far enough into the mysteries of economics to explain employment and unemployment at all adequately; but some elements of the explanation will be developed in Part III, below.

2. DISTRIBUTION AMONG OCCUPATIONS

What kinds of work do the people in the labor force do? This apparently simple question actually involves two questions: (1) How are workers distributed among the country's main industries? and (2) How many do each of the main kinds of work? The answer to the first question, and part of the answer to the second, as reported by the Census of 1940, is given by Table IV.

It will be seen at once that very close to half of the experienced workers were attached to industries fabricating material goods, the other half were concerned with getting these goods into the hands of users, and with the direct production of various sorts of services. During the war, the proportion of civilian workers concerned with material goods has been much higher; but 1940 is reasonably representative of peacetime conditions.

Looking across the line for 'all industries,' it will be seen that about one-fifth of the workers were self-employed 'employers or own-account workers' and about three times as many were employees earning wages or salaries in private employment (the remainder being government workers, persons working without pay for members of their own families,

TABLE IV

Experienced Workers in the United States by Industry and Type of Job: 1940
(millions of workers)

Industry group	All experienced workers	Workers with jobs, by type of job					Unemployed experienced workers, by type of job last held				
		Total	Employees on wage or salary — Private	Employees on wage or salary — Government	Employers or own-account workers	Unpaid family workers	Total	Employees on wage or salary — Private	Employees on wage or salary — Government	Employers or own-account workers	Unpaid family workers
Agriculture, etc.	8.9	8.5	2.1	*	5.2	1.2	0.4	0.3	*	*	*
Mining and quarrying	1.0	0.9	0.9	*	*	*	0.1	0.1	*	*	*
Manufacturing	11.5	10.6	10.2	0.1	0.3	*	0.9	0.9	*	*	*
Construction	2.8	2.1	1.3	0.3	0.5	*	0.7	0.5	0.2	*	*
Fabrication of material goods	24.2	22.0	14.4	0.4	6.0	1.2	2.1	1.8	0.2	0.1	*
Transportation and other utilities	3.3	3.1	2.8	0.2	0.2	*	0.2	0.2	*	*	*
Wholesale and retail trade	8.1	7.5	5.5	*	1.8	0.2	0.6	0.5	*	*	*
Finance and real estate	1.5	1.5	1.3	*	0.2	*	0.1	0.1	*	*	*
Professional service	3.4	3.3	1.3	1.5	0.5	*	0.1	0.1	*	*	*
Other service trades	5.8	5.3	4.2	*	1.1	*	0.5	0.5	*	*	*
Government	1.8	1.8	0.0	1.8	0.0	0.0	0.1	0.0	0.1	0.0	0.0
Industry not reported	1.3	0.6	0.6	*	*	*	0.6	0.6	*	*	*
All industries	49.5	45.2	30.1	3.8	9.8	1.4	4.3	3.7	0.4	0.2	*
Work relief	2.5	2.5	0.0	2.5	0.0	0.0	0.0	0.0	0.0	0.0	0.0

* Less than 50,000.

Detail does not in all cases add to totals because of rounding to nearest 100,000.

and workers 'on W.P.A.'). Besides the self-employed, however, a very large proportion of the employees had positions
of a good deal of independence and responsibility. Classification of the type of job by the type of work performed shows
the following (in millions):

Type of work	Total experienced workers (excluding work relief)	Employees, private or governmental	Self-employed or unpaid family workers
Professional and semi-professional	3.5	2.8	0.7
Farm managers	5.2	*	5.2
'Executive' and officials	3.8	1.7	2.1
Clerical, sales, and kindred workers	8.1	7.6	0.5
Craftsmen, foremen, etc.	5.6	4.8	0.8
All others	23.3	21.1	2.2
	49.5	38.0	11.5

As these figures suggest (and as the details of the Census
show still more clearly) it would be a great mistake to think
of the American working force as a large undifferentiated
mass with a few 'bosses.' Almost all the workers in the groups
specified above have skills and special status as workers
which they prize (often with fairly considerable property—
over 40 per cent of American families owned the homes they
lived in in 1940); and the same is true of a good proportion of
the 'all other' group. It is no accident that polls of public
opinion regularly find that most Americans consider themselves 'middle class' rather than 'working class.'

3. Efficiency in Occupational Distribution: Incentives in Choosing Occupation

It is a matter of the first importance for the economic organization of a community that its working population should
be divided among occupations in an efficient way. This means

not only that there should be the right number of workers in each occupation, but also that the qualities of the workers in each occupation should be as appropriate as possible—that people having particular capabilities should be in the positions where they can make the best use of their powers.

Now it is obvious that if each person worked in the occupation which he himself preferred to follow, just because he had a liking for that particular sort of work, this desirable distribution would not be reached; there would be far too many people in the more popular occupations, far too few in the unpopular ones. Some sorts of goods or services would be produced in much larger amounts than were wanted, while the supplies of others (some of which might be necessities of life) would be grievously short. The distribution of labor among occupations cannot be left to be settled according to the preferences of producers alone; the desires of consumers must also be taken into account. Since every producer is also a consumer, it is to everyone's interest that such an adjustment should be made.

There are two known methods of making the adjustment. One is the method of compulsion. The government may decide that more people are needed to work in a particular occupation; it may then pick certain people and compel them to transfer themselves where it wants them to go. Under the name of conscription, the method of compulsion is widely employed in war time; it may be the only practicable method of bringing about the immense temporary redistribution of occupations which is necessary to deal with an emergency such as modern war. Nevertheless, for normal purposes, it is distinctly less efficient than the alternative method. This alternative is to give people an incentive to transfer themselves to those occupations where the supply of labor is short. The incentive may take various forms. Certain kinds of labor are attracted into the British Civil Service by the prospect of honors (such as knighthoods), while in Soviet Russia the 'shock brigades' are said to have the best chance of theatre tickets or of being sent on holidays.[1] But the simplest form of incentive is to offer higher wages in those occupations where there is a scarcity of labor. People are encouraged to look for employment in those occupations where extra labor is wanted more urgently, in preference to occupations where extra labor is wanted less urgently, because they will be offered better wages in the former occupations.

Thus the use of the incentive method makes it almost inevitable that some people should get higher wages than others. But before we allow our sense of fairness to be outraged by these differences, we ought to consider very carefully what alternative exists. As we have seen, some means of regulating the distribution of labor among occupations is absolutely necessary; no community could survive without it. The only alternative is the method of compulsion. Now the method of compulsion is itself not beyond criticism on the score of fairness, and on other grounds it is distinctly inferior. Suppose that it is decided that 1,000 additional workers are wanted for some new trade, say the manufacture of radio sets; out of all the millions who are working (with more or less regularity) at other occupations, which thousand is it that ought to be transferred? The ideal solution would be to find those particular 1,000 people who will at once be the most useful in the new occupation and the least useful in their old occupations; and who can also be transferred from one occupation to the other at least trouble to themselves. These three tests (it should be observed that they are distinct and different tests) will not always be satisfied by the same people; yet clearly there will be some people who will satisfy the tests reasonably well, and some who will satisfy them very badly indeed. Clearly it is desirable that the people who are to be transferred should satisfy the tests reasonably well—but how are such people to be discovered? If the method of compul-

[1] Webb, *Soviet Communism*, p. 749.

sion is used without any adequate system of selection, then although the numbers transferred may be right, the choice of the particular people to be transferred will often be unsatisfactory. People will be transferred who would have been more useful at their old occupation, and also people for whom the transference involves exceptional hardship.[2] A means of selection is needed which will reduce the danger of these sorts of waste.

The great advantage of the incentive method is that it contains a means of selection within itself. When our employer in the radio industry is looking for his 1,000 workers, he estimates first of all what wages will be necessary to attract 1,000 suitable people. The rates offered will of course have to be high enough to attract a good many more than 1,000 persons altogether; the suitable people will have to be picked out of a longer list. But this is the only part of the work of selection which has to be performed by the radio manufacturer himself and by his managers; all they have to do is to select, out of the applicants who present themselves, those who seem best fitted to do the work which is to be done. Of course even this is not an easy job; but it is a job which people who are themselves specialized in the management of that particular kind of work will be specially competent to perform. They do not have to pay any attention to the other side of the selection; for the only people who will put in an application for work at a stated level of wages are people who consider that they will benefit themselves by getting employment on those conditions. There is thus no possibility of people being selected who would be involved in exceptional hardship by having to work at this job rather than at some other job

[2] When the method of compulsion is used in wartime, this sort of thing does of course happen; various more or less adequate devices have to be introduced in order to mitigate its consequences. Even so, these effects of compulsion are only tolerable because of the overmastering necessity of the tasks to which the labor is being transferred; they would be less tolerable in cases of less urgency.

which is open to them; such people will not apply. Neither is there much danger of people applying who are essential workers at other occupations; for if a worker who was really essential in his old job sought to change his occupation, his old employer would probably raise his wages, so as to make it worth his while to remain. It may indeed sometimes happen that a worker possesses some exceptional skill which makes both employers want him very badly; in that case he may be enticed away by the new employer offering even higher wages than the old employer would be prepared to offer. But if the new employer can only get this particular man by offering him exceptionally high wages, he has a strong induce- ment to do without him, if he can find any means of doing so. The method of incentive does give him an inducement to weigh up the urgency of his need against the need of the other employer, and not to take on a worker who is specially useful elsewhere unless he is also very specially useful in the new occupation.

4. LIMITATIONS OF THE INCENTIVE METHOD

The method of incentive has these advantages; if we con- sider how continually adjustments of this sort require to be made in a modern community, we shall appreciate how im- portant these advantages are. Yet we must never forget that the use of the incentive method does involve inequality of incomes. It means that those people whose abilities are more urgently demanded will earn higher wages than those whose abilities are less urgently demanded.[3] People who have no

[3] The resulting inequality is somewhat mitigated by taxing people's incomes at 'progressive' rates, which reduce large incomes by a larger percentage than small ones. This technique does of course somewhat weaken the incentive effect of differences in wages. But so long as equal treatment is given to all people at a given income level this weakening is not fundamental. For the incentive of high pay turns largely on pres- tige, and is more a question of the direction of the difference than of its precise size—particularly in high income brackets.

kind of ability which is at all scarce will earn relatively low wages; sometimes the wages they would earn would be so low that the public conscience is revolted by the idea of allowing them to work on those terms—if indeed they could earn enough to keep body and soul together. For this and other reasons, modern communities rarely allow the incentive method of distributing labor to operate unchecked and without qualification. Minimum wages are fixed in certain occupations, and unemployment pay is given to people who cannot secure work at these minimum wages. There is often a very good case on social grounds for making such arrangements; but when they are made it does mean that the actual distribution of labor among occupations will not conform at all exactly to the ideal standards we have been laying down. Unless the departure from these standards is absolutely necessary, it does involve a real loss in efficiency.

5. DIFFERENCES IN SKILL. INEQUALITY OF OPPORTUNITY

The differences in individual skill, which are mainly responsible for the differences in wages we have been discussing, come about in three ways—from differences in natural ability, in training, and in experience. A man can only be made into a first-class doctor or a first-class engineer if he has natural gifts for that sort of work, and if he has been properly trained. But even then he will only be able to use his gifts and his training to the best advantage when he has had experience in using them. Both training and experience take time to acquire, shorter and longer times in different occupations. In 'semi-skilled' jobs a worker can become proficient in a few months, while in professional and administrative work even those people who have the best natural endowments may not reach the height of their powers until after years of training and longer years of practice.

When a man's skill has been built up by years of training or experience, it is probable that he will be very much **better** at doing the work for which he has been trained, or which he has learned by practice, than he will be at any other sort of work. Unless he is given a very strong inducement to the contrary, the work to which he is accustomed is the work which he will prefer to do. At any particular time, a large part of the working population is specialized in this way on particular jobs; in regard to these people (so it might appear) the problem of distributing them into the right occupations hardly arises. But that is not altogether so, since the number of people who are specialized in a particular occupation at a particular time may be greater or less than the number wanted. In England, during the 1920's, there were too many coal-miners; as a result of the invention of more economical methods of using coal (by converting it into electricity, and so on) less coal was needed than before, and consequently fewer miners were needed. But while the coal industry was contracting somewhat, other industries were expanding. As a result of the improvements in motor-car manufacture, for example, more workers were needed in the motor industry than at any previous time. Not much could be done towards the necessary adjustment by transferring workers directly from mining to motor manufacture (the sorts of skill which were needed were too different). But workers were drawn into the motor trade from neighboring industries, workers who did possess kinds of skill more or less similar. These in their turn were replaced by others, and so, by a long process of shifting round, the supply of labor was fitted to the demand, the incentive to transference operating, in spite of specialization. Economic history is full of transformations such as this; they involve apparent wastage of what looks like valuable skill, but economic progress could hardly take place without them.

When the number of workers requiring to be transferred from one occupation to another is relatively small, the adjustment can usually be made in a smoother and simpler manner.

The people who are working in any occupation at any time will include beginners, as well as experienced workers. If it is only necessary for the beginners to move, a smaller amount of acquired skill has to be sacrificed. A smaller incentive will often be sufficient to induce beginners to move than will be needed if mature workers have to be uprooted. It is by influencing the decisions of beginners, and of new entrants to industry, that the most convenient way of adjusting the supply of trained labor to the demand for it is to be found.

When a boy is deciding what occupation to take up, he is bound to be influenced to a considerable extent by the sort of natural abilities he possesses (we most of us know very well that there are occupations we could never do useful work in, even in the most favorable circumstances); but in most cases he will also be influenced (or his parents will see that he is influenced) by the 'prospects' offered by particular occupations. These 'prospects' involve not only the wage which is offered at the moment, but also the assurance of regular employment, and of better wages when the job is learned. These things are more likely to be secured in a trade where the demand for labor is expanding than in one where it is contracting. Consequently careful decisions made on this basis do have the effect of directing labor towards those occupations where extra workers are most wanted.

There is however one other thing which has to be taken into account. The occupations which offer the best 'prospects' are usually occupations which require a long training. It is not surprising that this should be so, since most of the highest degrees of skill can only be acquired by the combination of long training with natural ability, and the necessity of a long period of training is itself a reason why the supply of such kinds of labor should be scarce. As things were until a few years ago, the opportunity of undergoing the longer periods of education and training was only open to the children of wealthy parents—and this limitation made the supply of such trained labor even scarcer than it would have been otherwise.

In the United States, educational opportunity is more generally accessible than in most countries. But in spite of the relatively low cost of training, and opportunities to live by part-time work and by the help of scholarships during the training period, many qualified people are prevented from learning the higher skills by sheer lack of money. Besides this, there are many trades and professions in which opportunities to learn the work are restricted to a small number of beginners, and either a connection with workers already established, or the 'background' of a successful family—or both—is required for admission. It is in this direction that the most serious inequality of opportunity still exists in our society; but to achieve a greater equality in this respect will not be an easy matter.

6. QUESTIONS LEFT OPEN

The questions which we have been discussing in this chapter are obviously controversial; they are also difficult, and it is not pretended that they are by any means exhausted by what has been said here. A large part of that more advanced part of economics which is called the Theory of Value is taken up with the closer analysis of issues such as those we have been raising. But although we shall have to return to such issues now and again, a systematic study of the theory of value lies outside the scope of this book.

VII

THE EFFORT OF LABOR

1. SUBDIVISION OF THE QUESTION

We have now discussed the numbers of the working population, and their skill; one further element in the contribution made by labor to the productive process remains to be dealt with—the effort which people put into their work. This is partly a question of the Hours of Labor, the proportion of their time which people spend in working; partly it is a question of effort in the narrower sense, of the energy and attention with which people work during their working hours. There are several economic questions which fall under each of these heads, questions which are particularly interesting from the standpoint of Industrial Relations and Labor Management. Only a few of them can be indicated very briefly here.

2. WORKING HOURS

It is usually the case that people will produce more if they work harder, but this does not mean that they will necessarily produce more if they work longer hours. After a certain point, the additional fatigue diminishes output. For any particular kind of work, there will be a certain length of working day from which a greater output can be secured than from any other length. If the number of hours worked is less than this critical number, production will be cut down because the workers have less time to work in; if it is greater, production will also suffer, because the additional time is offset by the fatigue.

The possibility that the working day may be too long for efficiency of production was demonstrated in a fairly unmistakable manner at the time of the early Factory Acts; it is a lesson which continues to impress the modern student of economic history, as it impressed Karl Marx.[1] Modern industrialists have learned this lesson reasonably well, and indications are that they do not often try to enforce working hours which are inefficiently long. It does occasionally happen in wartime that those who are responsible for the direction of industry are unable to resist the temptation of endeavoring to increase production by lengthening hours, even when there is in reality nothing more to be gained in that direction; but it is unlikely that mistakes of this sort are often made when pressure is less extreme.

The number of hours actually worked in normal conditions is usually appreciably less than the number which would give the maximum output. For this there is a very good reason. When the working day is at its most productive length, the fatigue which is imposed upon the worker is already nearly sufficient to cause a reduction in his output; it must therefore be already very considerable. It is not surprising that from their own point of view most workers would prefer to work rather shorter hours than this, and that they are even prepared to make some sacrifice in weekly or yearly wages in order to get shorter hours.

There has in fact been a notable shortening of the working week in most industrial countries during the last hundred years. During the 1840's and 50's it was the Ten Hour Day which was the objective of labor pressure; by the time of the last war it was the Eight Hour Day; by the 1930's, the Eight Hour Day having been widely secured, the objective moved to the Forty Hour Week. It seems highly probable that the main explanation of this long-continued tendency towards shorter hours is to be found in the general rise in the standard

[1] Marx, *Capital*, Vol. I, ch. 10.

of living which has taken place, more or less rapidly, over the whole period. As wages rise, people become prepared to make some sacrifice in weekly wages in order to get a little more time in which to enjoy the fruits of their labor. An increased supply of amenities, and even luxuries, can give little satisfaction if there is a shortage of time in which to enjoy them. Time and again, as the process of rising standards goes on, a further shortening of the working week becomes a thing which is even more urgently desired than a further rise in wages.

It is clear, on the other hand, that the conditions in which most industrial workers have to work are such as to make long hours particularly tiresome and trying. Those fortunate people whose work admits of much variety are not likely to mind very much how long they work; the only disadvantage which they get from working long hours is physical weariness. But when a man's work is very uniform and monotonous, his desire to have less of it may be very strong. It is not impossible that as people have become better educated, the irksomeness of factory labor has increased.

However this may be, there can be no doubt that the shortening of hours which has taken place during the last century (with some temporary set-backs during war emergencies) has been a great gain to labor. It is a gain which needs to be taken into account when measuring the economic progress achieved. The quantity of goods and services produced is not a sufficient measure of economic progress; if the same quantity of goods can be produced with a smaller expenditure of undesired effort, people will on the average be better off. Sometimes, even if there is a decline in the quantity of goods produced, the decline may be offset by a gain in leisure.

Instances of this sort do in fact occur. In 1919, at the end of the last war, there was in most British industries a rather sudden reduction in the length of the working week, a reduction which generally proved to be lasting. (The typical change was from a working week of about 52 hours before

1914 to one of about 47 hours after 1919.) Such a reduction
has to be taken into account when we are assessing the effect
of the war upon the productivity of industry. When we find,
as we do find,[2] that the quantity of goods produced per head
in Britain was in all probability just a shade lower in 1924
than it was in 1911, we must not conclude that productivity
was really any lower at the latter date. If there was any decline in the amount produced, it was certainly less than what
might have been expected from the reduction in hours. Economic progress had taken place, in spite of the war; but during these particular years, the gain from economic progress
had been deliberately taken out in the form of increased
leisure.

3. Effort and Application During Working Hours. Incentives and Rates of Pay

Much the same fundamental issues as arise in connection
with the length of the working day arise also in connection
with the effort and application of labor during working hours;
but the form which they take in practice is somewhat different. Just as the worker, looking (quite properly) at the
strain which is imposed upon him, will usually prefer to work
for rather shorter hours than those which would best suit his
employer from the point of view of production, so he will
often (though not always) prefer to work during his working
time with less intensity than his employer might desire. There
is a real conflict here, which inevitably causes trouble, though
we can see (when we look at the matter fairly) that it is not
in the least discreditable to either party. This is a conflict
more difficult to deal with than the parallel question about
hours. For it is possible to make an agreement about hours,
and to stick to that agreement over long periods. But the
effort which a man puts into his work is liable to vary, even
from day to day, for all sorts of personal reasons, so that it is

[2] Bowley and Stamp, *The National Income* 1924, pp. 56-8.

much more difficult to come to an agreement about it. Besides, effort is hard to measure objectively. The resulting situation can be dealt with, more or less satisfactorily, in one or other of the following ways.

The best way is to awaken the worker's interest in his work to such an extent that the conflict of interests is reduced to a minimum. We have seen that when a man is interested in his work, and feels a responsibility towards it, he is not likely to mind very much how long he works. Similarly he will not mind how much trouble he takes when he is working. A good employer may be very successful in awakening such a sense of responsibility, though usually he will only do so if he himself takes a good deal of trouble in watching over the welfare of his employees. Nevertheless, the success with which this policy is likely to be attended depends very much upon the character of the work which is to be done. Even the best employer will rarely succeed in arousing much interest when the work to be done is dull and monotonous.

The next best solution—in the case of repetitive work it is usually the best solution open—is to establish a connection between the intensity of work and the wages paid. This is called incentive pay. The simplest form of incentive pay is piece-work, according to which the worker is paid so much for each unit of the product which he turns out. The drawback to simple piecework is that the amount of product turned out does not always measure the intensity of work very satisfactorily. Quality may be important as well as quantity; a man's output may go up or down for reasons outside his control; one man's output may be larger than another's simply because of a difference in the equipment they are using. The methods of incentive pay which are adopted in practice have often to be adjusted so as to allow for these discrepancies; in the process of adjustment they may become very complicated indeed. Now complication is itself a disadvantage. Complicated methods are liable to rouse the suspicions of workers, who feel that they may be cheated by them. Indeed it is not unknown for both employers and workers to be cheated in these mazes, the system adopted having characteristics which damage the interests of both parties! The more complicated a system of incentive pay has to become, the less satisfactory (in most cases) it is; but the simpler systems will not fit the technique of production in more than a certain number of occupations without causing unfairness. There is thus a limit to the number of cases where the method of incentive pay can be conveniently applied. For several reasons the influence of labor organizations is commonly thrown against systems smacking of piecework, and in the United States payment on an hourly basis is definitely preferred by organized labor.

If neither of these two solutions is open—if the work to be done is in its nature uninteresting, and yet it is unsuited for incentive pay—then there may be nothing for it but to pay the worker by time (at a fixed rate per hour or per day, irrespective of output), and to bridge over the conflict of interests by the supervision of foremen or other managers. Obviously this method is less satisfactory than either of the others; it is only too likely to degenerate into petty tyranny, and it depends too much upon the sanction of dismissal. But there remains a considerable range of occupations (in the field of unskilled labor, for example) where no better incentive has been devised. It is highly desirable that this range should be narrowed; the best way to narrow it is by making improvements in the other methods, so that their application can be extended. The science which has particularly concerned itself with these improvements is Industrial Psychology; but the problem needs to be approached from the standpoint of economics as well as of psychology, if the happiest results are to be attained.

PART III

THE FACTORS OF PRODUCTION—CAPITAL

Part III

THE FACTORS OF PRODUCTION: CAPITAL

VIII

CAPITAL GOODS AND THEIR VARIETIES

1. CAPITAL GOODS AND THE CAUSES OF UNEMPLOYMENT

Capital, as we saw when we were making our earlier study of the productive process, consists of all those goods, existing at a particular time, which can be used in any way so as to satisfy wants during the subsequent period. Some of these goods are consumers' goods, which can be used to satisfy consumers' wants directly. Some of them are producers' goods, which co-operate with labor to produce further goods and services. When we are studying capital as a factor of production, it is mainly the producers' goods which interest us. In the present chapter and in that which follows it we shall concentrate most of our attention upon producers' capital.

So far we have divided producers' capital goods into two classes—durable-use goods and single-use goods. We shall now proceed to make a further subdivision. The purpose of this further classification is in part to improve our understanding of the nature of capital. But at the same time we shall find that it throws a good deal of light upon one of the most important of practical economic questions—on the causes of unemployment. Unemployment is of course itself a problem of labor; but the causes of unemployment have more to do with the factor of production capital than with the factor of production labor. Most of what can be said about the causes of unemployment within the framework of an introductory volume such as this will be found in the present chapter.

2. LAND

Durable-use producers' goods have generally been divided by economists into two classes, called (1) Land, (2) Fixed Capital. Land includes agricultural land and urban land (used for building sites and similar purposes); it also includes mines. Fixed Capital includes buildings, machines, tools, transport equipment, and so on.[1] The distinction between these two varieties of producers' goods received a great deal of attention from nineteenth-century economists, who used to mark their sense of its importance by classifying land as a separate factor of production, instead of treating it as a particular species of capital, which is the more modern practice followed here. All are agreed, however, that there is a distinction between land and fixed capital; what is the exact basis of the distinction?

Broadly speaking, we may say that Land (in its economic sense) includes those durable-use producers' goods which are given by nature;[2] Fixed Capital includes those which are made by man. More strictly, Fixed Capital consists of kinds of durable-use equipment whose supply can be readily increased, if we so desire, by the production of new units. Land consists of those kinds which are inherited from the past, and whose supply cannot be readily increased if we want more of them.

[1] Thus fixed capital does not mean fixed in location. The term is rather a curious one, having been borrowed by economists from accounting practice. Accountants, who have to look at economic problems from the point of view of an individual firm, think of the firm's 'capital' as the sum of money at its disposal. (We shall see in the next chapter how this fits in with the economic conception.) If a part of this money is spent upon durable-use equipment, it becomes 'fixed' for a long period—in contrast with money spent in purchasing materials, which is released again as soon as the materials are sold; thus the materials get the name 'circulating capital.'

[2] Land in the ordinary sense may be a consumers', not a producers', good. If it is used for gardens, or parks, or sites for dwelling-houses, it is a consumers' good.

It is not necessary to suppose that we could mark off, at all precisely, out of the whole equipment of a community existing at any particular time, just which items ought to be reckoned as land and which as fixed capital. Certainly if we attempted to do so by inquiring into the ultimate origin of each particular piece of equipment, we should raise some awkward historical questions, and should often be hard put to it to say what was man-made and what not. The agricultural land of England is presumably, for the most part, a free gift of nature; yet how much does it not owe to the improvements which have been made in it by successive generations of farmers, to the hedging and ditching carried out in the eighteenth century, and even to the clearing-away of the primitive forest by the ancient Mercians? The rich soil of Burgundy, on which the famous French wines are produced, is said by some of the best authorities to have been literally compounded out of the debris left by two thousand years of vine-growing.[3] But for the purposes of economic discussion, it is doubtful whether such historical questions as these need be raised at all. However the soil of England came into existence in the past, it is not possible to produce any more of it in the present. The most that can be done is to make improvements in its quality to a limited extent. Thus we may agree that in the economic sense it is land. The same holds, with minor qualifications, for the agricultural soil of the United States. In Canada and Alaska, on the other hand (as in past times in the United States), the next few decades may see a great extension of the cultivable area through improvements in transport and in the technique of living and farming in northern latitudes. Here the distinction between land and fixed capital is harder to draw. But the question is always

[3] 'C'est en fin de compte, non les vertus du minéral, mais les rudes labeurs humains, les misères et les peines de multiples générations de vignerons, qui ont fait, de ces sols ingrats entre tous, des terres de choix, de nobles crus, des lieux élus.' (G. Roupnel, *Histoire de la Campagne Française*, p. 249.)

whether human effort at the present time can increase the supply.

Durable-use producers' goods may also be classified according as they do or do not wear out as they are used. This basis of classification crosses that between land and other fixed capital. True, the great economist, Ricardo, described land (in a phrase which has become more famous than its author would probably have desired) as consisting in 'the original and indestructible powers of the soil.' [4] As we have just seen, the 'original' powers of the soil have been indistinguishably merged with the effects of drainage, fertilization, and other improvements. In many parts of the world (including the United States), farmers have learned from bitter experience that the powers of agricultural land are by no means indestructible. Ordinarily land *can* be so cultivated as to maintain its fertility. But there are few economic resources indeed which maintain themselves without human assistance.

Many types of natural resources—conspicuously mines and oil wells—cannot be used without being exhausted. Timber resources, while technically they can be maintained intact under use by careful forestry, tend in practice to be depleted—except in densely populated areas like western Europe, where the surviving timber is only that for which such forestry is profitable. Many types of capital goods, however well they are looked after, are unavoidably worn out after a term of years and require replacement. Replacement can often be postponed by suitable repairs (which in general means by replacing the parts of the machine or other structure piecemeal); but the time comes when repairs can no longer make the goods serviceable. Often this process is accelerated by 'obsolescence': even though a machine can be repaired to work as well as it ever did, it is more efficient to invest materials and labor in building a new machine of superior design rather than in rebuilding the old one.

[4] *Principles of Political Economy and Taxation* (1817), ch. 2.

It has become clear that the distinctions we have been trying to draw in the field of durable-use producers' goods are not easy to define very precisely. But they do enable us to distinguish an important class of durable-use producers' goods, which are such that a proportion of the existing supply must be expected to wear out every year, and which are also such that new units can be produced, as additions to the total supply, or as replacements for those which have worn out. Modern society is dependent upon the existence of such goods, but it is just this dependence which makes it so difficult to keep the economic system running smoothly. Let us see how that is.

3. Fixed Capital and the Capital Goods Industries. Irregularities in Production

The trades which specialize in the production of new fixed capital are called, loosely, the capital-goods industries. In terms of the occupational classification on page 80 above, they include workers in building construction and the greater part of the workers who manufacture goods made of metal, wood, clay, and cement. In most industrial countries such workers in recent decades have numbered from 10 to 20 per cent of the total working force. But in view of the enormous expansion in the metal-working trades produced by the war, it is highly uncertain where the proportion will settle when peace returns.

The capital-goods industries have the double task of constructing new fixed capital, and of replacing old fixed capital when it wears out. Let us take a numerical example in order to see how these two functions fit together. A certain community possesses, let us suppose, 1,000 ships; and let us say that a ship lasts, on the average, about 20 years. Then it would be possible, in completely steady conditions, to keep 1,000 ships constantly available by producing a steady output of 50 ships per year. Every year 50 ships would wear out, and every year there would be a new 50 ships coming forward to replace them. In 20 years the whole fleet would have been replaced—which is just the time it would take to wear out and to need replacing.

Now suppose that the community ceases to be contented with this constant number of 1,000 ships. In order to cope with the demands of an increasing population or of an expanding trade, the number of ships needed begins to expand at an even rate—say 3 per cent per annum. In order to have 1,030 ships in the second year, the number of new ships produced must be raised from 50 to 80. If 80 ships were produced every year, the total number of ships available would go on increasing in a regular manner.

This is more like the situation as it has usually existed in the actual world; but it should be observed that steadiness in the output of the shipbuilding industry now depends upon the expansion of the total demand for ships proceeding at a steady rate. And steadiness in *the rate of expansion* is obviously very difficult to attain. Population itself has not expanded at all steadily, though it has (up to the present) gone on expanding; but there are other things to be taken into account which are even less reliable. Inventions and changes in wants cause sudden accelerations and retardations in the demand for particular sorts of fixed capital. Political changes (particularly wars and their consequences) are even more disturbing. Even when economic progress is continuing without serious intermission, the rate of progress is liable to be speeded up or slowed down for all sorts of reasons.

Though these changes in the rate of progress may be quite moderate in themselves, they will have a considerable effect upon the activity of the capital-goods industries. We have seen with 80 ships produced every year, the numbers of ships available would go on increasing from 1,000 to 1,030 and 1,060 and so on. Now suppose that in the second year, the number of ships needed was a little larger than this. For the number of ships needed to be 1,050 instead of 1,030 would not imply any great disturbance in the demand for shipping. But if 1,050 ships were to be made available in that year, the number of ships produced would have to be 100, instead of 80. If in the third year no more than the normal 1,060 were needed, the number of ships produced in that year would only be 60 (10 as an addition to the total supply, and the usual 50 replacements). This means that if there were enough people specialized to shipbuilding to be able to produce 100 ships in the rush year, in the year after 40 per cent of them would be unemployed.

Nor is this all. We have so far been assuming that the existing supply of ships can be relied upon to wear out at a regular rate. If anything were to happen (as for example a war) which caused them to wear out, or to be destroyed, more rapidly than usual, the demand for new ships would obviously be further disturbed. There is also a more subtle reason why the rate of wearing-out may not be regular. If there have in the past been irregularities in the rate of production of ships, so that an abnormally large proportion of the existing ships were built in certain particular past years, the wearing-out of these ships is likely to be 'bunched.' Abnormally large numbers will need to be replaced during those years when the bunched ships are most rapidly wearing out.[5] We can now see a good many reasons why it is so difficult to maintain an even demand for the products of the capital-goods industries; and we can see that fluctuations in this demand are very likely to result in unemployment.

4. THE SPREADING OF UNEMPLOYMENT

There is no doubt that, as a matter of experience, the capital-goods industries do suffer from unemployment espe-

[5] This phenomenon has a good deal in common analytically with the effect of the age-distribution of population on birth-rates and death-rates, discussed in ch. IV, above.

cially badly. But the unemployment which arises from their instability does not affect the capital-goods industries alone, but spreads to other industries as well. For when these trades are slack, the people working in them have less to spend. The result is a slackening in the demand for other products. The unemployment disease is infectious: some trades get the infection first, and others catch it from them. The trades in which the infection originates are usually—though not always—the capital-goods industries.

The mechanism by which the unemployment virus is passed on is a very simple one. The incomes which most people spend are the incomes which they earn by working. If fewer people are working, there are fewer incomes to be spent, and fewer goods can be sold. Since fewer goods can be sold, fewer people are needed to make those goods, so that fewer people can be employed in those industries. This mechanism is not the fundamental cause of unemployment; it is the way unemployment spreads from one trade to another.

The spreading of unemployment is not impeded by national frontiers. Most people spend some of their earnings upon imported goods. When they have less to spend, they will buy smaller amounts of imported goods, as well as of other goods, and that will affect the foreign producers of these goods, causing unemployment in the countries where the foreign producers live. If we look at the matter from the point of view of these foreign producers, we can see how it will often happen that the unemployment infection may come into a particular nation from outside. So far as that particular nation is concerned, it is not its capital-goods industries which are primarily hit, but its export trades. Something of that kind has frequently been the experience of Great Britain.[6]

[6] At the time of the great unemployment in 1930-32 it was the experience of nearly all countries that their export trades were among the worst sufferers. This was a direct result of the protective policies so generally introduced. The government of each nation, finding that its people had less to spend, and that unemployment was therefore increasing

Most of these difficulties would be overcome if a means could be found for scotching the trouble at its source by achieving greater regularity in the output of the capital-goods industries. There are various ways in which this could be done—by replacing equipment at times when trade is slack, instead of at the time when it is technically most convenient to replace it, and so on. It is in this direction, far more than in any other, that the economic systems of modern communities are in need of centralized 'planning'; but planning a steady output of fixed capital goods can never be an easy matter. In practice, it is always bound to be complicated by political considerations. A great many of the capital-goods industries are capable of being turned over to armament manufacture, so that governments have an interest in them which is different from the economic interest, and may clash with it. These are some of the fundamental problems of the modern world.

5. WORKING CAPITAL AND INVENTORIES. IRREGULARITIES IN FLOW IN AND OUT OF INVENTORIES, AND EFFECTS ON PRODUCTION

Our classification of durable-use producers' goods has taken us far afield. Let us now see where we shall be led by the single-use goods. The distinction we have to make among single-use goods is also concerned with problems of the regularity of output; but naturally it takes a different form. The single-use goods in the hands of producers at any particular time, which we call Working Capital,[7] are partly goods ac-

among them, did all it could to induce them to economize on imports, rather than on goods produced at home; the result was to push the unemployment off on to foreigners, on to the exporting industries of foreign countries. With almost all countries behaving in this way, the exporting industries of all alike suffered.

[7] Also called Circulating Capital. In accounting terminology, Working Capital ordinarily means Inventories plus goods in process plus notes and accounts receivable from other firms, minus notes and accounts payable to other firms. Over industry as a whole, of course, the notes and

tually undergoing production—'goods in process' and goods being handed on from one stage of production to another. Partly they are stocks of materials which are not undergoing production at the moment, though they have been produced previously, and are expected to be used in further production later on; these we call Inventories.[8] We may think of the former part of working capital as symbolizing the regularity with which the greater part of the productive process does go on all the time, in spite of the ups and downs we have been discussing; but when we come to inventories we encounter some new sorts of irregularity.

If the wants of consumers never changed, but remained the same from day to day and from year to year, and if the outputs of goods never changed, it would be unnecessary for businesses to keep reserve stocks to any important extent. But since a manufacturer is often ignorant of the exact form which the next order coming to him will take, and since he usually needs rather different materials (different qualities, for instance) for dealing with different sorts of orders, he will need to keep stocks on hand, so as to be able to deal quickly with the orders that come in. Alternatively, the stocks may be kept not by manufacturers themselves, but by merchants, who are ready to sell without delay to any manufacturer who needs a supply. It is a very delicate problem of business management to decide what amount of goods needs to be held for this purpose. If bigger stocks are held, orders can be filled more quickly; it is a good thing for a firm's reputation to fill orders quickly, for by doing so it satisfies the consumers' wants better; but the holding of large stocks is very expensive. One of the easiest ways of economizing may be to let your stocks run down.

accounts cancel out (cf. ch. x), so that the total working capital of a country is substantially the same by either the accountant's or the economist's definition.

[8] This term is often used in a wider sense, covering goods in process.

Let us suppose that in a certain industry manufacturers (or merchants) are in the habit of keeping stocks of materials equal to the amount which is normally used in production during a period of three months. They may keep this stock by them for long periods, or they may 'turn over their inventory'—that is to say, every month they take one month's supply from their stock, and replace it by the same quantity newly supplied by the raw-materials producers. So long as this continued there would be no dislocation. But now suppose that these manufacturers decide to content themselves with smaller stocks, and that from now on two months' supply would be sufficient. In the month when this happened, they would take the usual amount from their stocks, but they would not give the usual order to replace what they had taken. During that month the demand for the raw material would be interrupted, although after the interruption it would continue as usual.

This sort of dislocation is worth considering, because it shows us that changes in the demand for the products of raw-materials-producing industries do not necessarily correspond at all exactly with changes in the purchasing of the ultimate consumer. The stocks which are held by merchants and manufacturers form a kind of buffer between the raw-material producer and the consumer for whom he is ultimately working. It is an elastic buffer, and it is liable to certain swellings and contractions of its own. A fall in business activity reduces the amount of stocks business men think necessary, which in turn accentuates the fall in activity. But the most important economic consequences of stock-holding arise when there has already been some disturbance in the production of raw materials.

There are many materials (for example wheat and cotton) which are the result of agricultural operations, so that supplies inevitably come in at certain particular times of the year. Since they are needed continuously and can be kept until they are wanted, merchants have built up a very delicate and ingenious organization to facilitate the holding of stocks on a large scale, so that supplies which only come in at particular seasons can be used at an even rate throughout the year. But it sometimes happens that this organization is subjected to exceptional strains. It can cope fairly well with the strain which is caused by a bumper crop, to which it reacts in the obviously desirable way of holding over the surplus in the expectation that on some future occasion there will be a shortage. But suppose (as is not unknown) that two bumper crops come in succession, what then? As warehouses become overcrowded, the costs of holding even larger stocks mount very rapidly, so that a signal has to be given to the farmers to cut down production. The same thing happens (and this has been a frequent occurrence in the modern world) if the demand for the product has been increasing very rapidly, but farmers have overestimated the rate at which it is increasing, so that they have produced more than the consumer is at the moment prepared to take. In either case the warehouses become loaded with *surplus stocks*.

It will be well for us to reflect for a moment on the situation which then arises, for there are few economic problems which in recent years have caused more misunderstanding. Either as a result of the vagaries of nature, or as a result of miscalculation, producers have turned out more than they would have desired to produce, and more than they would be willing to produce as a long-term policy in later years. If the commodity produced is a perishable one, there may be nothing for it but to destroy the surplus. Thus when there is an overproduction of fruit, the surplus has to be left on the trees, because the labor needed to convey it to market is not available. If the commodity could be stored very easily, it would be possible to hold over the surplus supply for a long period, releasing it very slowly in small quantities, so that little disturbance would be created as it was sold. Between these two extremes is the common case when the commodity can be stored, but storage is expensive; stocks can then be held over, but anyone holding a stock will desire to dispose of it as soon as he conveniently can. In this case there will generally be a period of two or three years after the surplus first occurred, during which it is being disposed of. During those years the demand for new supplies will be less than normal, since the wants of consumers are being satisfied to a considerable extent out of the surplus stocks. Thus these years are bound to be years of unemployment or of very low prices for the producers. It is not surprising that in some such cases (as in the famous case of Brazilian coffee after 1931) the producers should prefer to adopt the solution which would have to be adopted in the case of a perishable commodity—that is, to destroy the surplus! For by so doing they escape the awkward process of digesting the surplus stocks, which would otherwise hang over them for some time.[9]

The problems which we have studied in this chapter are very difficult problems; there is much more to be said about them than we have been able to say here. But further discussion of them would soon lead us into very advanced economics. It is sufficient for the present if we have appreciated some of the difficulties which inevitably attend the organization of a productive process which uses elaborate equipment. It should be observed that most of these difficulties are inherent in the productive process itself; they do not depend on the private ownership of capital. Some of the consequences of private ownership will be considered in the next chapter.

[9] On the question of Brazilian coffee, see J. W. F. Rowe, *Markets and Men*, ch. 2. The case for the policy adopted by the Brazilian government was much weakened when they continued the policy of destroying surpluses even in the years after the original over-production crisis was over.

IX

PRIVATE PROPERTY IN CAPITAL

1. The Transformation of Capital Ownership

If capital goods are to play their part in the ordinary running of the productive process, they need to be looked after. Someone has to be responsible for seeing that the durable-use varieties are kept in good condition, and that all kinds are used to advantage. In a socialist system, the duty of looking after the community's capital equipment would be exercised by public officials. In a system of private property, it is supposed to be performed by the private people who own the capital. There are some kinds of society for which the case which can be made along these lines for the institution of private property is extremely convincing; for instance, the great strength of peasant proprietorship as a form of land venture is to be found in the loving care which a peasant bestows upon land when it belongs to him. If capital is used to better advantage as a result of private ownership, and if the profits which are received by the owners are on the whole not more than a reasonable return for the care which they take of their property, then it may be more to the interest of the whole community (including those who are not owners of property) to have capital administered by owners, rather than by public officials (who would also require to be paid). But it is only possible to make out a good case for private ownership along these lines if the owners of property do actually look after the capital goods which they own. In practice it has become less and less true that they do so. The case for private ownership is in consequence considerably weakened; or at the least it is obliged to shift its ground. We shall give an outline in this chapter of the remarkable way in which the nature of capital ownership has been transformed during the course of the last two hundred years.

2. THE SINGLE ENTREPRENEUR AND THE PARTNERSHIP

The principal influence which has brought about this transformation is the growing advantage of producing on a large scale. New ways of producing on a large scale have continually been invented, and some of them have offered great gains in efficiency. Thus in many industries the size of the firm has had to keep on growing in order to take advantage of these more productive methods. In the middle of the eighteenth century a firm which employed a few dozen men was a large firm; when Arkwright in 1779 reached the point of having 300 employees it marked a decisive change, which we associate with the first stage in the Industrial Revolution.[1] By 1815 there were a few monster concerns whose employees were running into thousands. Although it was of course impossible for this rate of expansion to continue, we have today reached a point where firms with over a thousand employees are fairly numerous, while a few of the largest combines are well past the 100,000 mark.[2] Since the amount of capital used has generally increased more rapidly than the number of employees, even these figures do not fully reflect the change which has taken place. A change of this magnitude was bound to affect the whole problem of the control of capital.[3]

[1] Cf. A. Redford, *Economic History of England* (1760-1860), ch. 4.

[2] During the entire inter-war period the employees of the American Telephone and Telegraph Company and its subsidiaries numbered over 300,000; and the United States Steel Corporation in times of active operation is still bigger.

[3] It should be noticed that such changes in the scale of production, however they occur, are always likely to have repercussions in ownership. Many examples can be found in the history of agriculture. The English enclosure movement of the late eighteenth century is one of them; the collectivization of agriculture in Russia (the communist rev-

So long as the typical firm was only a small workshop with a handful of employees, the capital goods needed for production could usually be acquired by a single person out of his own possessions, though some part of them (perhaps the building itself) might be hired from someone else. If the business was successful, and earned good profits, some part of these profits might be used for the acquisition of more capital goods, and so the size of the business would grow. But excepting in very favorable conditions (such as did exist in the early days of the cotton industry, for example), the rate at which growth could proceed along these lines would be very moderate. The firm began small, and, even if successful, it usually stayed small.

In this primitive organization of business, the manager and controller of the firm, and the owner of the capital goods employed, were one and the same person. (Our ancestors referred to him as the 'undertaker' of the business. Nineteenth-century economists, fearing misunderstanding, preferred the French equivalent 'entrepreneur.') But when the advantages of producing on a larger scale began to develop, the capital goods needed for starting one of these larger businesses became too costly for a single person to be able to acquire them out of his own possessions—or rather, few of those people who possessed the right kind of ability were able to do so. A solution might, however, be found if a number of people clubbed together so as to provide the necessary capital equipment out of their joint resources. The legal form of this association was the Partnership.

Partnership is a system whereby a small number of persons hold capital equipment in joint ownership; and legally joint ownership is supposed to imply joint management. But in practice some of the partners will nearly always take a more active share in the administration of the capital than the

olution began on a basis of peasant proprietorship) was almost certainly another.

others do—the partnership is divided into active partners and
'silent partners.' Now the silent partner is putting himself very
completely into the hands of his associates. He is allowing
them to manage his capital for him, and on the success of
their management depends not merely whether he makes a
good income or not, but whether he preserves his capital or
loses it completely. To enter into a partnership when one does
not intend to take an active part in its management is a very
risky thing to do.

3. Borrowing and Lending: Capital Ownership in Paper Titles

It can readily be understood that there must always have
existed owners of capital who would be reluctant to enter into
partnerships. But there has always been an alternative method
by which the property of such people can be made available
for use in businesses which they do not control—the method
of borrowing. When an entrepreneur acquires the control over
capital by borrowing it, his obligations to the lender are set
down in the contract, which states that certain definite sums
of money are to be paid at particular dates, and so on. The
lender has no right to anything beyond what is laid down,
but to that he has a firm legal right. It is not surprising that
owners of property should often prefer to have a definite contract of this sort instead of the close association involved in
a partnership.

Capital may be lent in the form of goods, or in the form of
money. In the case of land or buildings, it is possible to arrange for a particular capital good to be leased or hired, subject to a precise agreement that it is to be returned in satisfactory condition; but (at least in ordinary business dealings) [4] it is not possible for single-use goods to be hired in
this way, since they are going to be used up in the process of

---

[4] Proviso made necessary by the American Lend-Lease Act (1941).

using them. There is, therefore, nothing for it but to express the loan in the form of a certain sum of money value, to be returned in money at an agreed date in the future. Even in the case of durable-use goods it is often more convenient for the loan to take this form. Instead of the borrower's being lent capital goods directly, he is lent a sum of money with which he can acquire the capital goods he needs.

The situation which arises as the result of a money loan such as this deserves very careful attention. If capital goods are owned by a partnership, then it is clear that the partners own those capital goods in joint ownership. If a landlord leases land or buildings to a tenant, then it is clear that the landlord still owns the property which has been leased; the tenant simply acquires the right to make use of the property. But if an entrepreneur borrows $10,000, and uses that $10,000 to make an addition to the capital goods under his control, these capital goods do not belong to the lender, nor to the lender and borrower in joint ownership. They belong to the borrower, and he has every right to dispose of them exactly as he wishes. But he does not personally become any richer as a result of this increase in the capital goods which he possesses (though of course he may become so in the end if he uses these additional resources advantageously). The increase in the capital at his disposal is offset by the debt of $10,000 which he owes. Similarly if the lender has sold capital goods (say house property) in order to be able to lend the $10,000, he is not made poorer as a result of his having a smaller amount of capital goods in his possession. The $10,000 debt owing to him stands in the place of the capital goods he sold. When we are considering the personal 'capital' of particular people, we have to regard the debts owing to them as part of their 'capital,' and the debts which they owe as deductions from their 'capital.' This is the reason for the distinction between *capital* in its economic sense (capital goods) and *capital* in its business sense (when it may mean nothing but pieces of paper acknowledging claims). The claims are indications that the control over capital goods has been transferred in return for the promise of an agreed annual payment.

If we contrast the position of a lender (who, after he has made his loan, is better described as a 'creditor' or 'bondholder') with that of a silent partner, we see that while the receipts of the silent partner are entirely dependent upon the way the business he participates in is managed, the creditor is bound to receive exactly what he has been promised, so long as the borrower is able to pay at all. The only risk to which the creditor is exposed is that the debtor will default on his obligation, and (at least so far as debts arising within a country are concerned) there is always legal machinery to ensure that debtors must pay if they can. But there is always the possibility that a debtor will not be able to pay (or not be able to pay fully), and a lender will therefore be more willing to lend if he has good reason for confidence in the *solvency* of the borrower. Since there are many cases in which the lender would himself be unable to acquire the requisite knowledge of the borrower's affairs, there is great scope for intermediaries between borrower and lender—intermediaries in whose own solvency the ordinary lender has confidence, and who can make the necessary inquiries before passing on the funds which have been entrusted to them. The work of these intermediaries is called Finance; there are various kinds of financial firms, but the most important are the Banks.[5]

One of the main considerations which a lender has to take into account when estimating whether it is safe to lend to a particular borrower is the amount of other capital which that borrower possesses. If a person who possessed no capital of his own tried to borrow $100,000, he would be unlikely to have much success. For even if the way in which he proposed

[5] The mutual relations of different kinds of financial intermediaries will occupy a good deal of the attention of a student of economics when he comes to the subject of Money.

to use the money appeared to be promising, the least mishap to his enterprise would leave him with capital goods worth less than $100,000, so that circumstances in which he would be unable to honor his obligations in full would be exceedingly likely to occur. Even if he possessed $100,000 of his own, the risk of losing half the capital invested in the enterprise would be quite considerable, so that a lender might still think that the security was not good enough. But if he already possessed a capital of $100,000, he would usually have little difficulty in borrowing an extra $10,000 for some promising purpose. For if capital goods to the value of $110,000 were used in a particular business, the chance of so much being lost that a debt of $10,000 could not be met would be relatively small. Whether it is a rule of economic affairs that 'to him that hath shall be given' may be disputed; but there can be no doubt that it is a rule of borrowing and lending that *to him that hath shall be lent.*

4. The Business Corporation

These two methods—partnership and borrowing—were the only legal methods of increasing the capital at the disposal of a single firm which were available (in ordinary cases) up to the middle of the last century. Even when they were both used to the utmost, there were limits to the amounts of capital which could be brought together in these ways. Partnerships did not work smoothly if they had more than half-a-dozen members or so; and the amount of money which could be borrowed by a partnership depended on the capital which the partners themselves were putting up. If (say) the partners themselves had contributed $100,000 and $100,000 had been borrowed, further borrowing might become very difficult, for the reason we have mentioned. The way in which these difficulties have finally been surmounted is by the formation of corporations, instead of partnerships, as a more convenient way of organizing large businesses; but before the 1850's the

only legal way of forming a corporation was by special legislation (as was done for the early railways), which was difficult
and expensive. So-called joint-stock companies were formed
in a less regular way, but these were in law nothing but extended partnerships, so that their legal position remained
anomalous and dangerous to their members.

The particular danger to which the members of these companies were exposed (the same danger besets all silent partners) was the danger of Unlimited Liability. The law de-
clined to make an absolute distinction between the private
property of a partner and the capital which he had contributed to the partnership. If the partnership was unable to
meet its obligations, the whole of the property of the partners
could be drawn upon to satisfy the demands of creditors.
Thus there was many a silent partner who experienced a rude
awakening; the business in which he had been mildly 'interested' suddenly collapsed and engulfed his whole fortune.[6]

The great change in the law on this matter was brought
about by a series of new acts, which have made it easy since
about 1870 to form corporations with Limited Liability. A
shareholder in a limited liability company is not liable for the
debts of the company to any greater extent than the capital
which he has contributed; thus if he has bought shares to the
value of $1,000, he may lose that $1,000 if the company is a
complete failure, but he cannot lose any more. The shareholder is therefore in a much less risky position than the silent
partner (whose role he in a sense inherits). There is nothing
to prevent the formation of companies with hundreds (or
even thousands) of shareholders, so that the amounts of capital which can be brought together by the company form of

[6] The potentialities of such a catastrophe as a source of domestic
drama were a godsend to novelists; but there was one novelist (Sir
Walter Scott) who experienced them in his own person. He had used
the profits of the Waverley novels to become a silent partner in a pub-
lishing house, which failed, leaving him personally in debt to the
amount of £130,000.

organization are much larger than what could have been brought together by partnerships.

It was perhaps not unreasonable for the law to assume that the members of a partnership would all be actively engaged in the management of their joint capital; but it would be obviously absurd to pretend that a crowd of shareholders could take any active part in the management of a giant concern, in which many of them would have no more than a few shares. The legal theory of the corporation is that the shareholders elect representatives—the directors—who administer their capital for them. In order to protect the shareholders against directors who might abuse their position, the law insists on safeguards such as a certain degree of publicity in accounts, and imposes penalties for the raising of capital on false pretences (misstatements in prospectuses, and so on). The history of company legislation is a long story of guerilla warfare between the law and a small fringe of ingenious rascals whose activities form the shady side of company promotion. On the whole the law has succeeded well in limiting fraudulent promotions; but it has been much less successful in enforcing the responsibility of management to the stockholders and the public.

The present status of business organization is roughly as follows: In farming and in small-scale merchandising, the single entrepreneur (using his own capital supplemented by borrowing) predominates. This is also true for the bulk of the 'service' trades—barber shops, etc., and in the professional field for medical and dental service. In all these fields partnerships are fairly frequent; and partnerships are typical in the law and in 'investment banking.' In small-scale manufacturing and the real-estate field an intermediate form between partnership and corporate organization is common—the small 'closely held' corporation, owned by only a few shareholders, and likely to be treated as a disguised partnership if legal problems arise. In England this intermediate form is legally recognized as the 'private company,' limited to 50 shareholders. Genuine corporations dominate large-scale merchandising and manufacturing, mining, banking, transportation, and public utilities. The chief determinant of the form of organization is plainly the amount of capital needed for operation of a unit large enough to be efficient.

5. Why Are People Willing to Be Shareholders?

The modern company has two ways of securing the capital goods which it needs in order to commence, or to expand, its operations: by borrowing, and by the issue of shares. The shareholders who have purchased the shares are in a certain sense part-owners of the company; they elect the directors, who are their representatives. But it is impossible for any legal provisions to give to shareholders the knowledge which they would need in order to elect competent directors;[7] so that in practice the directors of a new company are usually nominated before the shares are issued—before the shareholders have become shareholders—and they perpetuate themselves by co-opting others, whose selection is merely ratified by the shareholders. It therefore corresponds much more with the facts if we consider the directors of a company as themselves forming a kind of partnership, putting up some part of the capital themselves, and acquiring extra capital (often far in excess of what they have put up),[8] partly by borrowing,

[7] Just the same problems arise with political democracy. It is impossible for important officers, requiring specialized capacities, to be elected directly; for instance, a democracy which attempted to appoint its ambassadors to foreign states by direct election would soon be in a sorry plight. The method of electing general-purpose politicians whose business it is to make appointments, is not available in an association such as a corporation, itself formed for one specialized purpose.

[8] By the device of a 'pyramid' of 'holding companies,' control has in some circumstances been gained with very little capital. If an individual holds $51,000 out of $100,000 of voting shares in Corporation A, which in turn finances itself partly by borrowing and holds $201,000 out of $400,000 of voting shares in Corporation B, which similarly holds

partly by issuing shares. If we look at the matter in this way, we see that the issue of shares has itself developed into a kind of borrowing, distinguished from the other kind in just one significant way—that the bondholder has the right to a fixed payment (expressed as a fixed rate of *interest*), while the shareholder has no more than the right to a share in whatever *profits* are left over after other claims have been met.[9]

The shareholder has the protection of limited liability; but otherwise he puts himself into the hands of his directors, just as the silent partner puts himself into the hands of his associates. He gives over his property to the directors and lets them manage it for him, so that it depends on their ability and their diligence whether or not he gets a good return, or whether indeed he loses it altogether. At first sight it seems astonishing that shareholders should be found who will have such confidence in the directors of public companies, people with whom they are most unlikely to have any close acquaintance. The explanation is partly to be found in another consequence of limited liability. Since the shareholder cannot lose more than he has put in, whatever happens to the company in which he has invested, he will be in a safer position if he has small holdings of shares in a number of different companies than if he has 'all his eggs in one basket.' The silent partner could not thus spread his investments out without adding to his risks, but it is the common practice of the modern capitalist.

Another way in which the shareholder in a public company is protected is by the facility with which he can dispose of

$1,001,000 out of $2,000,000 voting shares in Corporation C. . . . , the original $51,000 acquires tremendous leverage in control. The law is now attempting to repress the use of this device, particularly in the electric-utility field, where it was excessively popular before 1929.

[9] Another thing which indicates that this is the right way of looking at the matter is the creation of various sorts of obligations intermediate between the bond (or debenture) and the *ordinary* or 'common' share—preferred shares and so on.

his shares whenever he desires. Shares in most companies can be bought and sold quite freely, without the company's officials being consulted in any way. In order to facilitate such transactions, there has grown up a body of dealers, who are organized in the Stock Exchange. The ability to sell his shares on the stock exchange does not indeed safeguard the shareholder against loss. If he gets bad news about the company, and so wants to dispose of his shares, the chances are that other people will have heard it as well, so that buyers will be hard to find, excepting at a reduced price. But the pessimist does get a chance of withdrawing his fingers before they get burnt too badly.

6. Does the Modern Capitalist Retain an Economic Function?

The final result of the transformation we have been describing in this chapter (a transformation, similar in outline, but with many tiresome differences in detail, has been going on in most other countries) is that the capital equipment of the community has, in the main, ceased to be owned directly by private people. The main exceptions to this rule (and they are only partial exceptions) are land and houses. It is a curious commentary on the attitude often taken by social reformers towards land ownership that the modern landlord still performs a real function in looking after the capital goods in his ownership, while most other owners of capital hardly do so any longer. They have mostly given up their direct command over capital goods and acquired titles to ownership, which are only pieces of paper, without any particular goods being identifiable to which they correspond. Since the shares owned by the modern shareholder are usually spread over a number of different companies, his connection with any particular capital goods has practically disappeared.

This is indeed less true for company directors themselves, who are usually important shareholders in the companies they control, and it is less true for the shareholders in small companies. In these cases something of the original function of ownership remains. But if we ask what economic function is retained by the purely passive shareholder, it can be no more than the function of enabling the active directors and controllers of business to get command over capital. Now it is a real advantage that they should be able to do this easily, because it enables new opportunities for the expansion of business to satisfy consumers' wants to be seized upon easily, and (above all) to be seized upon without delay. The facility of raising capital is actually increased by the looseness of the connection between the particular capitalist and any particular set of capital goods. For if a business desires to raise more capital it is not obliged to appeal to those particular people who happen at the moment to have spare money available. It has the much wider choice of applying to anyone who possesses shares which can be sold on the stock exchange, and who would be willing to sell some of these shares and lend the proceeds to the business in question. This facility of raising capital is a real social gain, though the full possible advantage is not always taken of it. But perhaps it is not a large gain to set against the considerable part of the social output which has to be set aside for the payment of interest and dividends, and against the possibility of acquiring power without responsibility.

We shall be returning to this point when we come to consider the Distribution of Income;[10] it will suffice for the present if we have got some idea of the remarkable evolution which has been taking place in the institution of Private Property—an evolution which is probably not yet finished, and which may yet have some surprising turns in store.

[10] See below, ch. xvii.

X

THE NATIONAL CAPITAL

1. ASSETS AND LIABILITIES

We have now examined the nature of capital under two aspects: (1) its aspect as a factor of production, consisting of real goods being used in the productive process; (2) its aspect as a superstructure of rights and titles to ownership, by means of which the real goods are linked up with their ultimate owners. The general way in which these two aspects are fitted together is becoming clear. The capital possessed by an individual capitalist will usually include some actual goods (houses, land, durable-use consumers' goods, and so on), but for the most part it is likely to consist of paper titles, shares and bonds. These latter cannot be associated with particular pieces of real equipment, but are claims against the equipment used by firms; usually they entitle their holders to receive interest or dividends out of the profits which the firms earn by using that equipment. Now since a company, from the point of view of ownership, is simply a means whereby a number of people can hold capital goods in common, the capital equipment of the company, after other obligations have been met, belongs to its shareholders. The conventional way of expressing this when drawing up a company's accounts is to reckon the shares as *liabilities* of the company, and to bring out the company's liabilities as equal in value to its *assets*. (The assets of a company—like those of an individual person—consist of the property it possesses, plus the debts due to it; its liabilities are the debts which it owes, or the claims

which are set against its assets.) This would work out in a
concrete case in the following way.

Suppose that the company has been formed in the year
1935, and its capital was then got together by issuing ordinary shares to the value of $1,000,000 and by borrowing
$300,000 on debentures or bonds. Let us suppose that we are
considering its position at the beginning of the year 1938.
At that time it also owes $100,000 to a bank, and $50,000 to
various trade creditors (goods have been delivered to it, but
not yet paid for). On the other side it is owed $50,000 by cus-
tomers who have not yet paid for the goods which have been
delivered to them; and it possesses equipment, consisting of
the various sorts of real goods, valued at $1,500,000. The re-
sulting situation would be expressed on a balance-sheet more
or less as follows:

Assets		*Liabilities*	
Equipment (including land, buildings, plant, goods in process, materials and finished products on hand)	$1,500,000	Notes payable to banks	$ 100,000
		Accounts payable to suppliers	50,000
		Bonds outstanding	300,000
		Capital stock	1,000,000
		Surplus	100,000
Accounts receivable from customers	50,000		
	$1,550,000		$1,550,000

The firm has been a moderately successful one, so that the
total value of its assets exceeds the value of its debts *plus* the
original value of its share capital. This leaves a balance of
$100,000, appearing as 'surplus' on the liabilities side, because
any such surplus accrues to the shareholders, and is available
to be distributed to them in dividends (though a prudent
management will not begin to distribute any such surplus
until it has grown fairly large). Nevertheless, we may say
that the ordinary shareholders, who originally contributed
$1,000,000, now have claims worth $1,100,000. (If the firm

had been unsuccessful, the balance might have gone the other way, and the claims of the ordinary shareholders would be worth less than what they had originally contributed.)

When the balance-sheet of a company is understood in this way, it will be seen that it is quite proper for the two sides of the account to add up to the same figure; for if the claims of shareholders are treated as liabilities, the *net assets* of the company (assets *minus* liabilities) must of course be nil. In the case of a private individual, on the other hand, net assets are normally a positive amount. A private person may owe some money to his bank, and he may have bills owing to shopkeepers which at a particular moment he has not yet paid; but these liabilities are nearly always a good deal less than his assets, for the very good reason that he would be unable to give adequate security for loans to any larger amount. We shall be considering one exception to this rule a little later on; [1] but such exceptions are of little practical importance.

2. The Connection Between Economic Capital and Business Capital

Let us now take a simple case, and see how the two aspects of capital fit together. Suppose that we have a company like that we have been considering, but with no trade debts either way, and no debt to a bank. Let us further suppose that its shareholders (including bondholders) have no investments in other companies. Then we can take the company and its shareholders together, and can treat them as a self-contained group. The total capital of the group can be added up in two different ways, either of which will give the same result.

On the one hand, we can look at the capital from the side of ownership. The shareholders will have in their private possession certain capital goods (houses and so on) which have no connection with their investments in the company. Let us

[1] See below, pp. 130-31.

say that the value of these personal possessions is $200,000. They also own shares and bonds to the value of $1,500,000. If we assume that they have no personal debts, their total net assets come to $1,700,000. The net assets of the company are, as we saw, zero. Therefore the net assets of the whole group are $1,700,000.

On the other hand, we may look at the real goods. The shares and bonds worth $1,500,000 correspond, in the company's books, to real equipment worth $1,500,000. Writing the company's balance-sheet in an abbreviated form, and subjoining a similar account for the shareholders' private possessions, we get the following table:

Assets		*Liabilities*	
Company: Capital goods	$1,500,000	ª Shares and bonds	$1,500,000
Shareholders: Capital goods	200,000		
ª Shares and bonds	1,500,000		
Company and shareholders together: Capital goods	1,700,000		

When company and shareholders are taken together, the paper claims (marked ª) cancel out, giving us the sum of the possessions of the whole group, nothing but the real equipment, which is worth $1,700,000, the same as the total value of the net assets.

The reason why the paper claims cancel out is that we have added together the capital of the company (for which the claims are liabilities) and the capital of the shareholders (for whom they are assets). If we were to take any group of individuals and institutions, and were to perform a similar addition, we should find that all debts and obligations *between members of the group* cancelled out in the same way, appearing as positive items in the accounts of some members and negative items in the accounts of others. If the group were a self-contained group, not having any debts or claims excepting between its members, the total capital of the group could be estimated, either by adding together the net assets of all members, or by adding up the values of all the real capital goods possessed. The two totals would have to come out to the same figure.

3. THE NATURE OF THE NATIONAL CAPITAL

The particular group for which it is most interesting to make such a calculation is, of course, the Nation. When we add together all the assets and liabilities of all the persons and institutions which compose a nation, most of the paper claims (being owed by firms to persons, or persons to firms, or firms to firms, or persons to persons, all of which are included in the nation) cancel out in the way we have described. If the nation were completely self-contained, we should find that when we had made the cancelling-out properly, the sum of the net assets of all the persons and institutions in the country gave us the same total value as the capital goods possessed by the nation and its citizens. Very roughly, this is what we do find; but there are a few snags in the cancelling-out process which need a little attention.

First of all, a modern nation is not a completely self-contained group in the sense which would be needed for the cancelling-out to be perfect. Firms engaging in foreign trade will generally have debts owing to foreigners, and will be owed debts by foreigners; while some of the nation's citizens will be shareholders in foreign companies, and some of the companies operating within the country may have foreign shareholders. In consequence, if we were to add together the net assets of all the members of a national group, we should find that the cancelling-out process was not complete. There would be loose ends in the form of paper claims owed to or by persons outside the nation. Since the accounts of these outsiders would not be added in to the national reckoning, the claims to which they were parties would only appear on one side of the national balance-sheet, instead of cancelling-out by appearing on both.

The capital account of a nation would thus have to be written in the following form:

Assets	Liabilities
Real capital goods	[a] Obligations due to fellow nationals
[a] Obligations due from fellow nationals	Obligations due to outsiders
Obligations due from outsiders	

The National Capital of a country equals the sum of the net assets of all individuals and institutions within it. This is the difference between total assets and total liabilities. Since the obligations ([a]) to fellow nationals cancel out, the national capital (as appears from the table above) equals the total value of all capital goods possessed by members of the nation, *plus* the excess of obligations due from outsiders over obligations due to outsiders. Thus most of the national capital consists of real goods; but in the case of a creditor country (such as Great Britain has been, at least until lately) something has to be added on to the value of these real goods to allow for the investments which its citizens have made abroad; while in the case of a debtor country, such as Australia, something has to be subtracted from the value of the capital goods owned by Australians or by companies operating in Australia, in order to allow for the shares in these companies owned by non-Australians, and for other debts owed overseas.[2]

4. THE NATIONAL DEBT

The other main snag in the cancelling-out process arises over the National Debt. In order to see how this fits into the calculation, let us begin by taking another rather similar case, of infinitely less importance, but easier to understand.[3] A young man who expects to inherit some property on the death

2 We shall be returning to the subject of foreign investment in ch. XII.
3 This is the case to which we referred above, p. 127.

of an elderly relative can sometimes succeed in borrowing money from a money-lender without any security but his 'expectations.' The practice is not a wise one, and it is probably much less common today than it was in the aristocratic society of earlier times. But how does it fit into our accounting? The loan, when it has been made and spent upon riotous living, is an asset to the money-lender and a liability to the gilded youth who borrowed it. It is not a liability to the elderly relative, from whose estate it is expected to be paid; he has not been consulted about it at all, and would be within his rights if he cut the spendthrift off 'with a shilling.' Thus there are no capital goods outstanding against the loan; we cannot regard it as a claim possessed by the money-lender against any of the real capital goods of the community. But, being a debt from one member of the nation to another, it has to be cancelled out when we are adding up the national capital. There is nothing for it but to regard the net assets of the spendthrift as a minus quantity, a state of affairs which is only possible because he has the expectation of getting an addition to his assets at some future date which will enable him to pay his debts.

Apart from a few special cases such as this, no individual or firm can have negative net assets. If a person's liabilities became greater than his assets, he would be adjudged bankrupt, and his assets would be divided up among his creditors, each of them receiving as many cents on the dollar as the assets would provide. Governments, however, can have negative net assets without going bankrupt, and can carry on in that situation for an indefinite period; the reason being that they have the power of raising taxes to cover the interest on their debts.

The national debts of governments have been mostly accumulated by past wars. However necessary these wars may have been, they are unlikely to have resulted in the acquisition of capital goods as industrial borrowing would do; there is nothing to show but the immaterial gains of freedom and independence. Whatever may be the case from a higher standpoint, the situation of the government, when the war is over, is from the standpoint of national accounting just like that of the spendthrift. It owes a vast debt, and has no assets to set against it. Its net assets are negative.

When we are setting out the national balance-sheet, the national debt has to be reckoned as a liability of the government. If the people to whom the debt is owed are themselves citizens of the country, it will appear as an asset in their accounts; and so, when the accounts are added together, the national debt cancels out, like other internal debts. It is only when some part of the debt is due to foreigners that there is no cancelling out; external debt of this sort is a genuine deduction from national capital. From all points of view, a large external debt is much more damaging to a nation than a large internal debt.

5. ESTIMATES OF NATIONAL CAPITAL. THEIR LIMITATIONS. NATIONAL CAPITAL OF GREAT BRITAIN

Now that we have discovered how the capital of a nation is made up, let us turn to the figures, and see how it works out in a particular case, that of Great Britain.[4] Table v gives an estimate of the capital account of Great Britain at some date in the years 1932-4; something not very dissimilar would hold for any date between 1932 and the outbreak of war in 1939. But before this table is even approached, it is necessary to utter a most solemn warning. The information which is available for making an estimate of the national capital of Great Britain is much less good than that which can be used for most other large-scale economic calculations. (It is much less

[4] Available national wealth statistics for the United States do not at present (1945) permit putting a parallel calculation on a reliable basis. It is hoped that work in progress at the National Bureau of Economic Research will remedy this deficiency within the next few years.

good than that which we shall use for the calculation of the national income in Part IV below.) The proportion of guess-work in calculations of the national capital is abnormally high. This is partly because of defects in our information which could conceivably be remedied; direct information about many of the items is lacking, so that estimates have to be made by roundabout and imperfect methods. But the fundamental cause lies deeper, and can hardly be removed in the nature of the case.

The greater part of the national capital consists of durable-use goods, land and buildings, vehicles and machines. What value is to be put upon these goods? It should be noticed, in the first place, that any one of these goods has, in ordinary practice, two sorts of values: (1) its *capital value,* the value at which it could be sold outright; (2) its *annual value,* the price which would be paid for the right to *use* it during a year, the article to be returned in good condition when the year is over. Since most of these durable-use goods are expected to last for much more than a year, their capital values will usually be much higher than their annual values. The selling price of a house, for instance (which is its capital value), will usually be from 10 to 15 times as high as the rent, which is its annual value.[5]

For the purpose of calculating the national capital, the values which are used are capital values, not annual values.[6]

---

[5] The relation between the capital value of an article and its annual value does not depend entirely upon the number of years the article is expected to last. Even in the case of land, which is more or less expected to last for ever, the selling price is rarely more than 20 times the rent. The selling price of a promise by the British Government to pay the same sum in interest every year for ever is now (1941) about 30 times the interest (or annual value); that is, the rate of interest (annual value divided by capital value) is a little over 3 per cent.

[6] The annual values of capital goods reckon into the national output, not the national capital. We have seen that the rents of houses (the price paid for the use of house-room) are part of the value of the social output.

TABLE V

The National Capital of Great Britain, 1932–4
(*millions of £'s*)

	Assets		Liabilities		Net Assets
Private persons, including farmers	Houses	3,500	[a] Due to building societies, &c.		......
	Other durable-use consumers' goods	700		500	
	Agricultural land	600			
	Farm equipment	400			
	[c] Government Debt	2,500			
	Foreign investments	1,500			
	[b] Shares, bonds, and other obligations of British firms	14,000			
Total property of private persons		about 23,000		500	22,500
Firms	Buildings and land	1,000	[b] Shares, bonds, and other obligations	14,000	
	Railways	750			
	Other industrial and commercial equipment	8,000			
	[c] Government Debt	3,500			
	[a] Mortgages on house property, &c.	500			
	Gold	250			
Total property of firms		14,000		14,000	0
Government and other public bodies	Land and Buildings	600	[c] National Debt	6,000	
	Other equipment	1,400			
Total public property		2,000		6,000	−4,000
Total National Capital					18,500

But to arrive at the capital value of a durable-use good is often not an easy matter. When a house is sold for $10,000, we can say without any hesitation that its capital value is $10,000; but many of the durable-use goods which are included in the national capital will not have been sold since long before the date to which the calculation refers, and their owners will not be proposing to sell them (if at all) until long after that date. What value is to be put upon such goods? There are several purposes (in connection with the inheritance of property and with certain kinds of taxation) for which it is necessary to value these goods; skilled valuers are trained to do the job, but the methods which they use vary according to the purpose for which the valuation is wanted. The fixed capital used by a manufacturing firm may have half a dozen

(Note to Table V)

The figures in this table are based on H. Campion, *Public and Private Property* (Oxford University Press, 1939), particularly pp. 65 and 84. In order to fit Mr. Campion's figures into the accounting form suitable for our purposes, I have had to make some extra guesses, which do not claim to be more than guesses, though I think they are reasonable. (1) Mr. Campion gives £4,600 millions for the total of private houses and buildings used for business purposes taken together. I have divided this, with an eye on the valuations for taxes. (2) The Colwyn Committee estimated that holdings of the national debt were divided between firms and private persons in about equal shares; holdings by firms were probably larger in 1932 than in 1927, so I have made an adjustment to allow for this.

The following points should also be noted: (1) Armaments and roads are not allowed for in Mr. Campion's estimate of public property. The reader is at liberty to make an addition to the national capital to allow for these, if he so chooses. (2) The foreign investments included among the national assets are net obligations due from outsiders. Material property owned by British firms in other countries (branches, subsidiary companies, &c.) is included among the material assets of firms. (3) The external debt of £1,000 millions or so to the American Government was not being paid after 1931, so it is neglected. An American would be within his rights if he deducted £1,000 millions from our estimate of the national capital on account of this debt. (4) Gold in the Exchange Fund has been added to gold in the Bank of England; but that makes it all the more of a question whether both of these institutions should not be reckoned among *public bodies*, rather than among *firms*. It should be noted that these stocks of gold were largely increased during the years 1933-8. (5) Holdings of national debt by public bodies are cancelled out, so they do not appear in the table.

different values which can plausibly be put upon it. Different values may be put (1) by the directors and managers of the firm, (2) by their shareholders, (3) by another firm which might consider purchasing the whole equipment 'as a going concern,' (4) by yet other firms who would only be willing to purchase the equipment bit by bit. In addition to these there are the values at which the same capital might be assessed for purposes of taxation, central and local, which are not necessarily the same as any of the preceding. In any estimates of the national capital these last values, made for taxation purposes, have to be drawn upon to a large extent, because they are the most readily available; but it should be noticed that they may have less economic significance than some of the others.

The estimate of the national capital which is given in the table on page 134 is thus an exceedingly rough estimate; it does not claim to do more than give the right impression. For this reason the figures are given in very round numbers. More is to be learned from the general layout of the table and from the relative importance of the various items than from the actual figures themselves.

The table can be added up in the two ways which have been indicated. On the one hand, we may proceed by considering the net assets of the three groups. The net assets of private persons (the total of private property) come to £22,500 millions; the net assets of firms are of course nil; the net assets of public bodies are *minus* £4,000 millions. This gives us £18,500 millions for the national capital. Alternatively, we may strike out all those items (marked [a, b, c]) which occur both in the liabilities and in the assets columns; if we then add up the remaining assets, we shall again get £18,500 millions. If we adopt this second method, we have the advantage of seeing how the national capital was made up in these years 1932-4; it included real capital goods to the value of about

£17,000 millions and obligations due from outsiders worth about £1,500 millions.

One interesting point which emerges from the table is the place of money in the national capital. Modern money consists in the main of obligations from one member of the nation to another; thus a pound note is simply a statement of debt from the Bank of England to the holder of the note. We are reckoning the Bank of England as a firm, so that the bank notes held by private people count among the obligations marked (ᵇ) in the table. Similarly, when a person has money in a bank, all that exists is a debt to him from the bank, so that also counts under (ᵇ). On the same principle, money held by firms is to be reckoned as a debt from one firm (the bank) to another, so it has already been cancelled out, like other debts between firms, and does not figure in the table explicitly. Silver and copper coins are a little more complicated, but since the metal contained in these coins is worth much less than the face value of the coins, it is best to regard them also as a kind of notes, printed on metal instead of paper so as to wear better. The only kind of money which comes into the final reckoning as part of the national capital is the gold held by the Bank of England (or the Government); there is no doubt that this gold must be included, because it can be sold off to foreigners (if so desired) and useful capital goods got in exchange for it.

XI

THE SOCIAL OUTPUT AND THE SOCIAL INCOME

1. Contrast Between Social Capital and Social Output

The general picture of the productive process during any period, which we worked out in Part I of this book, and have needed to keep at the back of our minds throughout our later discussions, can be briefly described as labor working on capital to produce output. In Parts II and III we have discussed the factors of production—labor and capital; now we come to the Social Output. We shall devote a good deal of our attention to the problem of measuring the social (or national) output, mainly in order that we should have a clear idea of what the social output consists, and what are its component parts. When we have done this, we shall be in a position to say something about changes in the social output, how they are caused, and how people's economic welfare is affected by them.

There are many similarities between the problem of measuring output and the problem of measuring capital; we shall meet again over our new problem some of the same difficulties as we have met already. But it is very important that we should keep the two problems clearly distinct. Both the output of a community and its capital consist, for the most part, of a collection of goods (though output contains services as well, while capital does not). But the goods which are included in the one collection are not the same as the goods included in the other. The goods included in capital are those which exist at a particular moment of time; the goods included in output are those produced during a period of time.

Some of the goods contained in output are durable goods, which will also count as parts of the community's capital at any time when they are simultaneously in existence. A house finished in April and a house finished in June are both in existence in July, and will count as parts of the community's capital in July. But a loaf of bread baked in April has been eaten before a loaf baked in June comes into existence; both loaves are part of the year's output, but there is no date at which they are both of them parts of capital.

Thus the social output consists of a different collection of commodities from that which makes up the social capital; but they are both of them collections of commodities including many different sorts. Because of the different sorts of commodities included in capital, the only feasible way of reducing them to a common basis, so as to get a single figure for the national capital, was to take their values in terms of money (this quite apart from the question of foreign debts). We gave figures for the national capital as so many dollars and just the same has to be done for the national output. We must always think of the social output as consisting of goods and services, things useful for satisfying wants; but when it comes to measurement, the only way of adding together an output consisting of so much bread, so many bicycles, so many ships, so many hours' teaching, and so on, is to take the value in terms of money. There are serious defects in the money measure, so that it has to be used very carefully. But we shall find it convenient to begin by taking the money measure for granted, leaving its defects, and how they can be remedied, for later discussion.[1]

2. IDENTITY BETWEEN SOCIAL OUTPUT AND SOCIAL INCOME ESTABLISHED IN A SIMPLIFIED CASE

The methods of computing the social output which are commonly employed depend on a very important economic prin-

[1] See below, ch. xv.

ciple, which is concerned with the close relationship between the value of the net social output and the total of the incomes of members of the community. When this principle is applied, as we usually want to apply it, to calculating the output of a nation, there are a couple of snags which complicate the argument; after our study of the national capital, the reader will not be surprised to learn that these snags are due (1) to the existence of obligations to and from abroad, (2) to the economic activities of the government. We shall deal with these snags in due time,[2] but for the present it will simplify things if we leave them out of account. In the rest of this chapter we shall make the unreal assumptions that there are no economic relations with persons or bodies outside our community, and that the economic activities of the State can be neglected. When these assumptions are made, the argument is easier to follow; there is not much harm in making simplifications of this sort if we propose to fill in the gaps later on.

Subject to these assumptions, the principle we have to establish is very simple. It states that the value of the net social output of the community and the sum of the incomes of its members are exactly equal. The social output and the social income are one and the same thing.

It will be convenient to begin with a special case in which this principle is directly obvious. Let us suppose that the whole of the productive system of our community is organized in a single giant firm, which controls all the capital equipment, and employs all the labor. This is very much the situation which would exist in a perfectly socialist community; the whole economic system of such a community would consist of a single firm, in which the State would own all the shares. We need not here suppose that the State owns the shares, as we do not want to bring the State into the picture just yet; we will suppose that the shares belong to a body of

[2] See below, chs. xii and xiii.

private shareholders, who may thus be regarded as the indirect owners of the capital equipment.

The net social output and the net output of our Firm are then one and the same thing. It consists, as we know, of the total amount of Consumption Goods and Services produced, *plus* net Investment, which is the increase in capital equipment brought about by the year's production. The wages of labor have to be paid out of the value of this output; but all the rest is profit, belonging to the shareholders.[3] The wages of labor are the incomes of the laborers; the profit left over is the income of the shareholders. The value of the social output is thus equal to Wages *plus* Profits; and Wages *plus* Profits equals the sum of incomes. The net social output equals the social income.

The same equality can be tested out along another route, by considering the way in which the incomes are spent. People will spend part of their incomes on buying consumption goods and services (buying them, of course, from the Firm, so that a part of its output is accounted for in this way); the rest they will save. Now when we say that a person saves a part of his income, we do not mean that this part of his income is not spent; saving is the opposite of consumption, not the opposite of spending. When a person saves, he uses a part of his income to make an addition to his assets; he is still saving, whatever form the additional assets take. Thus one possible way for a person to save would be by purchasing new equipment directly, and adding it to the assets in his possession at the end of the year. If we supposed that all the savings took this form, then it would be easy to see that the social income would purchase the social output. The part of the social output which consisted of consumption goods and services would

[3] Since our firm controls the whole of production, there can be no purchasing of materials from other firms.

be bought out of consumption expenditure; the part which consisted of the net investment would be purchased out of savings. Income as a whole would purchase output as a whole; we should have social income equaling social output along this route too.

Further, it is obvious that the equality would not be disturbed if we were to suppose that the savers, after acquiring the new equipment in this way, did not retain it in their possession, but lent it back to the Firm. The social income would still have purchased the social output; but the Firm would retain control of the new equipment, issuing shares in exchange for it. The additional assets of the savers would now take the form of shares; the shares would be a liability to the Firm, but the Firm's assets and liabilities would still be equal, as they should be, because the Firm would have the new equipment, equal in value to the shares, added on to its assets. The Firm's balance-sheet would still balance.

In order to arrive at this last situation, it would obviously be unnecessary for the actual goods which constitute the new equipment ever to pass directly into the hands of the savers. The savers might use their savings to acquire shares directly, and the Firm might issue the shares for them to acquire, without the new equipment ever changing hands. If the value of the shares issued was equal to the value of the savings, it would also be equal to the value of the net investment. The Firm's assets and liabilities would still balance; the savers would have acquired shares to the amount of their savings, while the goods which constitute the net investment would be retained by the Firm and added to its capital equipment.

So long as we assume that the whole of the capital equipment of the community is controlled by the single Firm, it is this last form which we ought to suppose the saving to take. People save by acquiring shares in the Firm; but the creation of the shares is only the reverse side of the accumulation of additional equipment by the Firm. When a person saves, he acquires the right to receive some part of the profit which will be earned by using the additional equipment which is being produced. He uses a part of his income to acquire a share in the indirect ownership of that new capital equipment.[4]

Let us look back at the combined balance-sheet of firm and shareholders, which was given in the last chapter,[5] and see how it is affected by saving. Taking figures more appropriate for a giant Firm, we should have at the beginning of the year

Assets (billions)		*Liabilities (billions)*	
Firm: Real equipment	$100	Capital stock, etc.	$100
Shareholders: Shares of stock in firm	$100		

At the end of the year we should have

Assets (billions)		*Liabilities (billions)*	
Firm: Real equipment	$105	Capital stock etc.	$105
Shareholders: Shares of stock in firm	$105		

The extra $5 billion of shares held by the shareholders are their savings; the extra $5 billion worth of real equipment is the net investment. Since the Firm's assets and liabilities must be equal *at both dates,* the savings must be equal in value to the net investment.

[4] A particular person may indeed dispose of his savings in another way than by lending them to the Firm: he may lend them to another private person and so enable that other person to consume in excess of his income. But we need not pay much attention to lendings of this sort, for when the borrower and lender are taken together, the saving obviously cancels out. There is no excess of total income over total consumption. It is only savings which generate such an excess which are genuine savings; under our assumption of the single Firm which owns all the capital equipment, such genuine savings must be lent to the Firm.

[5] P. 128.

Thus the fact that people save by acquiring titles to the ownership of parts of the new equipment, instead of by acquiring new equipment directly, does not disturb the relationship between the social output and the social income. That relation can be summed up in the following very important equations:

On the earning side

$$\begin{matrix} \text{Social} \\ \text{Output} \end{matrix} = \begin{matrix} \text{Wages} \\ + \\ \text{Profits} \end{matrix} = \begin{matrix} \text{Social} \\ \text{Income} \end{matrix}$$

On the spending side

$$\begin{matrix} \text{Social} \\ \text{Income} \end{matrix} = \begin{matrix} \text{Consumption} \\ + \\ \text{Saving} \end{matrix} = \begin{matrix} \text{Consumption} \\ + \\ \text{Net Investment} \end{matrix} = \begin{matrix} \text{Social} \\ \text{Output} \end{matrix}$$

These equations will remain valid in spite of all the further complications which we shall take into account in the rest of this chapter. But in the two following chapters we shall encounter certain points where it is necessary to take some care over the interpretation of these equations.

3. COMPLICATIONS: UNDISTRIBUTED PROFITS, HOUSE RENTS, DIRECT PERSONAL SERVICES

It will be convenient, as a next step, to take into account some complications which can be allowed for while still supposing that industry is organized in a giant Firm.

In the first place, we have hitherto been assuming that the Firm pays out to its shareholders the whole of the profits which it earns, that the shareholders then save part of the incomes they get in this way, and that they lend these savings back to the Firm. In practice, a firm might be inclined to short-circuit this process, and to keep back part of its profits, instead of distributing all the profits to the shareholders directly. In such a case, what effectively happens is that the shareholders are compelled to save a part of the incomes which are due to them; additional shares may not be issued, but the shares previously outstanding will increase in value, because of the additional capital goods which they represent. The undistributed profits have to be reckoned as a part of the social income; they are really part of the incomes of the shareholders, although they are not usually counted as such, because the shareholders do not get them into their own hands. They have to be reckoned into that part of the social income which is saved; there is a part of net investment corresponding to them, as there should be.

Secondly, we have been assuming hitherto that private people can hold in their personal possession no sort of capital goods, not even consumers' capital goods, such as houses. If we allow them to possess such things as houses, then the rents of these houses have to be reckoned as part of the social income, income derived from a form of capital which is not in the possession of the Firm. (It will be remembered that we are reckoning the use of the houses as part of the social output.) Expenditure on paying the rents of houses is of course a part of consumption. The building of new houses is a part of investment; we may suppose that the actual building is carried out by the Firm, but the part of its output which consists of new houses is sold off to private people, just as the consumption goods are sold off, and not lent back to the Firm, like other investment goods. If private people spend some part of their incomes in buying new houses, they are adding to the assets which they will have in their possession at the end of the year, just as they would do if they acquired shares; consequently income spent in buying new houses is a part of saving. The new houses are to be looked on as a part of new equipment, which is retained in direct private ownership, and not handed back to the Firm in return for shares.

Thirdly, we have been assuming that all labor is employed by the Firm. This is not very convenient in the case of some of the direct personal services, such as medical care and domestic service. If we allow some of the people who provide direct services to be working on their own account, not for the Firm, we have to distinguish a part of the social output, consisting of these services, which is not part of the output of the Firm, and also to distinguish a part of the earnings of labor which are not wages paid by the Firm. The income spent on these services is a part of consumption, so it finds its place in the table without any difficulty.

Let us now consider what alterations have to be made in our equations to allow for these three complications which we have been discussing. On the earning side, instead of Wages *plus* Profits, we must write Earnings of Labor *plus* Profits *plus* House Rents; and these in turn can be further divided up. So we have the following equivalent columns:

Social Output	Net Output of Firm *	Wages paid by Firm *	Earnings of Labor	Social Income
		plus	*plus*	
		Profits of Firm * paid out to shareholders	Profits of Capital	
			plus	
			House rents	
		plus		
		Undistributed * profits		
	plus	*plus*		
	Services of Labor not employed by Firm	Earnings of Labor not employed by Firm		
	plus	*plus*		
	Use of house-room	House rents		

On the spending side, consumption and saving can be similarly divided up, so that we have as our other set of equivalent columns:

Social Income	Consumption of goods produced by Firm *	Output of consumption goods and services	Consumption	Social Output
	plus Consumption of other labor services			
	plus Consumption of house-room			
	plus Saving spent on buying new houses *	plus Output of new houses sold to savers		
	plus Saving lent to Firm *		plus Net Investment	
	plus Saving in the form of un-distributed profits *	plus Net new equipment of Firm *		

These expanded tables are exactly the same in principle as our earlier tables. They still show the social income being earned in the production of the social output, and being spent in buying the social output.

4. COMPLICATIONS: TRANSACTIONS BETWEEN FIRMS

We are now in a position to drop our assumption of the giant Firm. In the tables we have just given, the part played by the giant Firm is exactly the same as that played in reality by all the firms which compose industry and commerce, when they are taken all together. Our Firm is simply the whole collection of actual firms rolled into one. And we can see the part which this whole collection of firms actually plays in the earning and spending of the social income, by looking at the place of the single Firm (marked out by the starred items) in the above tables. On the earning side, the net output of the Firm is equal to the wages it pays out, *plus* its profits (distributed and undistributed). On the spending side, the net output of the Firm is purchased (1) out of consumption expenditure, so far as it consists of consumption goods; (2) out of saving, so far as it consists of new consumers' capital goods, such as houses; (3) out of saving, so far as it is offset by lending to the Firm; (4) out of saving, so far as it corresponds to undistributed profits. This is the position of the single giant Firm, as it appears in the tables; but this is also the position of the whole collection of firms, which compose the real world of industry and commerce, *when they are all taken together*. This we shall now proceed to show.

The new points which emerge when we pull apart our giant Firm into the multitudinous separate firms, large and small, which correspond to it in reality, are only two in number. On the one hand, we have to take account of the materials and equipment [6] which are produced by one firm and sold to another, which uses them in its own production. These materials and equipment do not come into the picture, so long as industry and commerce are supposed to be amalgamated into one single Firm, because the passing on of materials from one stage of production to another is then a purely internal matter within the Firm. When the firms are pulled apart, the sale of materials looks just the same to the firm which sells them as any other sort of sale does. But since we have also to take into account the purchase of the materials by the firm which uses them, the sale and purchase of such materials will cancel out when all firms are taken together.

The other point which has to be taken into account when

[6] There are also certain services, such as transport and insurance, which are performed by one firm for another, so that their role is similar to that of materials.

we have more firms than one is the possibility that a part of the shares (or other obligations) of one firm may be owned, not by private persons who are shareholders, but by another firm. If this happens, a part of the profits of the one firm will be paid out to the other firm; but here again, when all the firms are taken together, these transferences of profits will cancel out. The only profits left will be those which are actually paid out to private persons, or which remain as undistributed profits. A further consequence of this possibility is that savings lent to one firm may not be used as a means of increasing the capital goods in the possession of that firm, but may be lent again to some other firm. (An obvious example of this is the case of the banks.) These re-lendings, too, will cancel out when all firms are taken together.

5. THE PROFIT-AND-LOSS ACCOUNTS OF FIRMS AND THEIR PLACE IN THE SOCIAL INCOME

Thus the separation of firms makes absolutely no difference to our general argument. All transactions between firms cancel out, when all firms are taken together, as they have to be for calculation of the *social* income or output. But it will nevertheless be instructive to show in detail how the cancellation proceeds, by looking at the way in which firms do actually calculate their profits in practice. Firms calculate their profits by drawing up a profit-and-loss account; what we have now to show is the way in which the profit-and-loss account of a particular firm finds its place in those general accounts of the whole community, whose nature we have been investigating in this chapter.

The profits which are earned by a firm from the production of a particular year equal the value of its output *minus* the expenses to which it has been put in order to produce that output; but in the case of a firm which has obligations (shares or bonds) owing to it from other firms, the interest or divi-

dends received from these other firms may also make a contribution to the firm's profits. The expenses of producing output include (1) wages and salaries; (2) cost of materials used
up in order to produce the output; (3) cost of services, such
as transport and insurance, provided by other firms; (4) depreciation of the fixed capital equipment.[7] The profit left over
after these expenses have been covered belongs to the owners
of the firm's capital equipment, or to people who have lent
money to it with which the equipment has been acquired;
thus some parts of the profit may have to be paid out in rent [8]
of land or buildings (hired directly), or in interest on borrowed money; what remains is available for distribution to
the firm's shareholders, though a prudent management will
usually not distribute the whole of the residue, but will keep
back some part of it to add to reserves.[9]

A typical profit-and-loss account could therefore be set out
in the following form, which is substantially equivalent to
that used in practice (the figures are only for purposes of
illustration):

[7] Some discussion of the problems involved in measuring depreciation
will be found in Appendix, Note C. In practice, certain taxes (for
example, local property taxes) will count among the expenses of production; but we are postponing the consideration of such questions as
taxation.

[8] In practice, it would be more usual to reckon the rent of land or
buildings as an expense, rather than as part of profits. But since rent-
ing is nothing but an alternative way of getting control of capital
equipment (the firm might have borrowed money and purchased the
land or buildings outright), our tables will come out more neatly if we
reckon the rent as a part of profits.

[9] It is of course possible that in a particular year the expenses of
producing the firm's output may be greater than the value at which the
output can be sold; a firm which is in this position will make a *loss*,
not a profit. Losses are usually met by drawing on reserves; in this case
the contribution made by the unlucky firm to the 'undistributed profit'
item in the table on p. 154 will be a negative, not a positive, quantity.
Strictly speaking, that item should read 'undistributed profits *minus*
business losses.'

Value of output	$1,000,000	Wages and salaries	$500,000	
		Cost of materials	200,000	
		Transport, insurance, etc.	25,000	Expenses
		Depreciation	75,000	
Interest and dividends received from other firms	50,000	Rent of land or buildings	50,000	
		Interest to bondholders	50,000	Profits
		Dividends to shareholders	100,000	
		Undistributed profits	50,000	
	$1,050,000		$1,050,000	

Since the two sides add up to the same figure, we can rearrange this account in another way, which is more convenient when we want to be able to consider all the firms in a community together. The account which follows has identically the same significance as that just given.

Value of output		$1,000,000	Wages and salaries		$500,000
less			Profits	$250,000	
Cost of materials	$200,000		*less*		
Transport, insurance, etc.	25,000		Interest and dividends received from other firms	50,000	
Depreciation	75,000				
		300,000			200,000
		$700,000			$700,000

This new way of writing the account has the advantage that the columns now add up to a total which is of great economic significance. The $1,050,000 to which the first account added up is not a figure which would have any significance except to the firm itself; the $700,000 which comes out as the total when the account is written in the second form is the net output of the firm [10]—its contribution to the net output of the community. If the accounts of all firms were written in the second form and the totals added together, we should get as a result the net output of all firms together—the net output of industry and commerce, which corresponds to the net output of the giant Firm in our previous tables.

We can check up this correspondence on either side of the account. On the right-hand side, the net output of the firm is wages *plus* profits *minus* interest and dividends received from other firms. When all the net outputs are taken together and the totals added up, the parts of profits which are paid out to other firms will cancel out against the corresponding receipts by the other firms. The only profits which will be left are those which are paid out to private persons (shareholders, bondholders, or landlords), and those which remain as undistributed profits. The net output of all firms taken together is thus equal to

> Wages and salaries
> *plus* Profits paid out to private persons
> *plus* Undistributed profits

But the total of these is just what the total of wages *plus* profits would be if industry were organized as a giant Firm; and we have seen that this is equal to the net output of industry and commerce.

Now look at the left-hand side. Here we have a similar cancelling-out to perform, because of the services performed by one firm for another, and because of the materials sold by one firm to another. The transport, insurance, etc., which figure among the expenses of production for most ordinary firms, are part of the output of such firms as railway companies and insurance companies, and cancel out against that output. Materials which are produced by one firm within the

---

[10] This is frequently called the 'value added' by the firm.

year, and used up by another firm within the year, are reckoned in the output of the first firm and in the cost of materials for the second; thus they also cancel out when the firms are taken together. But some of the materials which are produced during the year will not be used during the year, but will be added to stocks; some of the materials used during the year will not have been produced during the year, but will be taken from stocks. Thus *all* materials will not necessarily cancel out.

When we have performed the cancellations, the sum totals of the left-hand sides for all firms taken together will come out as follows:

	Value of output of consumers' goods
plus	Value of new fixed capital produced
less	Depreciation of fixed capital
plus	Value of materials added to stocks
less	Value of materials taken from stocks

which can also be written

	Value of output of consumers' goods
plus	Net investment in fixed capital
plus	Net investment in stocks of materials

This is easily recognizable as the net output of consumption goods and investment goods produced by industry; that is, it is the net output of industry as before.

Thus the net output of industry and commerce is equal to the sum of the wages and profits derived from industry and commerce; and the other elements in the social output (direct labor services, services of houses) have already been accounted for. Subject to the assumptions which we made at the beginning of this chapter, the equality between social income and net social output seems to be fully checked up.

6. Methods of Calculating the National Income

The methods which are commonly used by statisticians for the calculation of the national output (or national income) now suggest themselves at once. Although there are certain corrections which have to be introduced when the simplifying assumptions are dropped (we are going to discuss these corrections in the following chapters), the connection between net national output and the sum of incomes remains close enough for it to be possible to approach the same problem from either side, from the side of output or from the side of income.

The most direct approach is the *income payments method,* which proceeds either by estimating the total amount of different types of income or by estimating the incomes received by persons of different types. In the United States, the total of income payments is built up by estimating total payrolls (including salaries), dividends and interest reaching individuals, net cash rents reaching individuals, and net profits of farmers and other self-employed, and a few minor items. From this total of 'income payments to individuals,' national income can be estimated by making adjustments for undistributed corporate profits, for non-cash rents, and for certain government transactions.[11] In Great Britain, where the statistical source material is different in character, income is estimated for wage-earners, for persons liable for income tax, and for non-wage-earners not liable for tax; from the resulting total, national income is estimated by making adjustments for undistributed profits and for double-counting in the total. In principle a national total could be arrived at by making a field study to find the number of incomes in each range of income size, and adding the incomes so found; in practice such studies are so hard to carry out and the results are so imperfect that the total so derived is only a very rough check on the income payments total.[12]

[11] See ch. xiii, below.

[12] A carefully designed and executed study of this sort made by the government in the United States for 1941 showed very incomplete reporting of property income and a considerable under-reporting of wages

The second method is the census of production or *commodity flow* procedure, which begins from the output end instead of the input end. This consists in estimating net output either by industrial group or by type of final product. The standard American estimates on this basis have been compiled by using statistics on the flow of basic materials to gauge the flow of finished consumption goods and investment (or in the private language of American income estimators, net capital formation). On the consumption side, commodity flow estimates yield in the first instance estimates of output at farms and factories, which have to be raised by an allowance for the final stages of production (i.e. transportation and marketing) and lowered by an allowance for business use of such commodities as gasoline which appear both as producers' and as consumers' goods. These figures have to be supplemented by figures for consumption services taken over from the expenditure estimates to be discussed in a moment; and sometimes expenditure figures are substituted for commodity flow figures in the sphere of consumers' commodities. On the investment side, estimates are made of the total output of producers' durable-use goods and housing, and of the growth in inventories of other goods; this sum is called Gross Capital Formation. From this sum is subtracted an estimate of wear and tear on durable-use goods and housing (Capital Consumption), yielding Net Capital Formation (i.e. Investment) as a residual. Statistically this estimate is independent of that made by the income-payments method, and serves as control; for the United States the two methods give very similar results.

The third method is the *expenditure* procedure. This relies

and salaries; the aggregate found was more than 10 per cent below a corresponding figure from Department of Commerce income payments estimates. Similarly, the 1935-6 study of incomes by size showed less than the Department of Commerce, and the 1940 Census data for wages and salaries earned in 1939 also fell low.

on retail trade data [13] for consumption estimates; and instead of estimating net capital formation it involves estimating the amount of saving in different forms. For the present, savings estimation has not been systematized in a way that lends itself to this use; so that the consumption component is used chiefly as a substitute for a commodity flow estimate, and is combined with capital formation estimates to yield a hybrid estimate of social output. As with the income-payments approach, there is a possibility in principle of determining the amounts spent and saved in various ways by persons in each income-size group and combining the results; but adequate data are not at hand.

We shall examine the results of some of these investigations later. But first we must discuss the qualifications to the statement that net national output equals the sum of the incomes of members of the nation. We shall begin with the question of external relations.

[13] Minus estimates for goods sold at retail which are for business use rather than consumption, such as automobiles bought for salesmen, gasoline bought for trucks, coal sold at retail for heating shops, etc.

XII

FOREIGN PAYMENTS AND THE NATIONAL INCOME

1. Creditor and Debtor Nations

So far as the total amount of the national income is concerned, only one alteration in what we have said has to be made when economic relations with other countries are allowed for; and this alteration is already implied in our study of the national capital. The social capital of a self-contained community consists of the goods possessed by its members; the social income of a self-contained community is derived from the output of labor working on those capital goods. Thus, for a self-contained community, social income equals net social output. But the national capital of a nation [1] may include not only goods but also obligations due from outsiders; in this case, the members of the national community will derive incomes from the interest or dividends on these foreign assets, as well as from the net national output. [2] Or, on the other hand, it may be that the members of the nation have obligations owing to outsiders, on which they have to pay interest or dividends; if so, a part of the net national output has to be paid to outsiders, and only what is left over

[1] In this account the 'nation' will be treated as including resident aliens and excluding non-resident citizens.

[2] Meade and Stone, in their fundamental article on the classification and presentation of national income material (*Econ. Jour.*, 1941), prefer to maintain the equality between *National Income* and *Net National Output* by reckoning income from foreign assets as a part of output. Though we have already stretched the idea of output very far, when we included in it such things as the services of houses, the further extension involved in the Meade-Stone definition seems to the present writer intolerable.

after these payments have been made remains to form the incomes of the nation's own members.

If the obligations from outsiders are greater than the obligations to outsiders we say that the nation is a *creditor nation.* A creditor nation has a national capital which is greater than the value of the capital goods used in its own productive process, and it has a national income which is normally greater than its net national output by the net amount of interest and dividends received from abroad. In the reverse case, a *debtor nation* has a national capital less than the value of the goods used in its own productive process (less by the amount of its net foreign *liabilities*); and it has a national income less than the value of its net national output by the net amount of interest and dividends which it has to pay to outsiders.

The debtor-creditor relationships between different nations have an extraordinary importance in the modern world; changes in them produce vast economic and political repercussions. Before 1914, the great creditor nations were Great Britain, France, and Holland (it was no accident that these were also the great colonial powers); Germany was also a creditor nation, but to a less degree. Among the debtor nations were almost all the Americas, Russia, the British Dominions and India, China, and Japan. The results of the War of 1914 were to weaken the creditor positions of Great Britain and France, to transform the United States from a debtor into a creditor, to transform Germany from a creditor into a debtor, and to produce new debtors among the smaller countries of central Europe. Russia defaulted on her debts after the Communist revolution, and Germany ceased to pay on hers at the time of the Nazi revolution.

It is too soon (in 1945) to say precisely what results the present war will have on international debts; but already after five years of war, Great Britain has disposed of foreign assets and acquired new overseas liabilities to such an extent as to make it doubtful whether she will be able to retain her position among the creditor nations when the war is over. Since the passage of the Lend-Lease Act early in 1941, the United States also has been moving away from its creditor position, building up a considerable debt to raw-material producing countries in Latin America, which under war conditions cannot be supplied with industrial equipment, etc., which they wish to import. In the immediate postwar period, however, it is not unlikely that both countries will again lend heavily abroad.

Some of the effects of these transformations will appear as we go on; but before we can approach these great matters it is necessary to re-work some parts of the argument of the last chapter, so as to see how foreign trade, as well as foreign obligations, is related to the earning and spending of the national income. Fortunately it will not be necessary to go over the whole ground again; the necessary adjustments can be made fairly easily.

2. The Balance of Payments on Income Account

Let us go back to the fundamental equations of pp. 149-50. On the earning side we have no alterations to make, excepting that we must allow for the foreign assets and liabilities already mentioned. For a creditor nation, the earning equations will be:

Net National Output   =   Wages   =   National Income
plus Net income from foreign assets   *plus* Profits

The spending side, as usual, is more difficult.

The incomes which compose the national income may be either consumed or saved; but now we must distinguish how they are consumed and how they are saved. The part of income which is spent upon consumption goods may be spent on consumption goods produced at home, or on consumption goods which are imported; we must further remember that even when an article is supplied by a home manufacturer, imported raw materials have often been used in the making of it. It is only such part of the value of these goods as corresponds to the use of home labor and capital which must be reckoned as consumption of home products; the rest must be included among the imports.[3]

This, then, is how consumption is divided up; what about saving? As we have seen in the last chapter, the saving performed during a year corresponds to the additions made to the national capital during that year; but these additions may now take two forms—additions to the equipment of real capital goods possessed by the community (Home Investment) and additions to the foreign assets (Foreign Investment). Further, the capital goods added to the initial equipment may have been produced at home, or they may have been imported.

Thus we have, on the spending side,

National Income = Consumption = Consumption of goods produced at
       plus   home
       Saving   *plus*
              Consumption out of imports
              plus
              Net Home Investment out of goods
               produced at home [4]
              plus
              Net Home Investment out of imports [4]
              plus
              Savings lent abroad (Foreign Investment)

In order for our equations on the spending side to square with those on the earning side, the last column must add up

[3] It is only the materials imported *during this year* which must be reckoned as imported; materials imported in earlier years were part of the initial equipment at the beginning of the year. Thus, so far as this year is concerned, they count as coming out of home capital.

[4] The using-up of initial equipment in home production must be deducted from the part of the investment which is produced at home, while any export of initial equipment must be deducted from the investment out of imports.

to the same total as that of net national output *plus* net income from foreign assets. Now if we look down the list of items appearing in this last column, two of them (the first and third) are obviously themselves parts of the net national output. These two items cover that part of the net national output which is used for home consumption and home investment. When they are subtracted from the net national output, what is left? Nothing but that part of the net national output which is exported.

Thus, in order for the tables to square, the following columns must come out equal:

Consumption out of imports	= Home produce exported
plus	*plus*
Net investment out of imports	Net income from foreign assets
plus	
Savings lent abroad	

This last is a very important equation: it is called the *Balance of Payments on Income Account*. With a little rearrangement, it can be turned into a still more important equation, called the *Balance of Payments* without qualification.

3. THE BALANCE OF PAYMENTS PROPER

The balance of payments on income account has been set out in the form which is appropriate for a creditor country which is continuing to lend abroad, so that both the net income from foreign assets and the savings lent abroad are positive quantities. In the case of a debtor country, the net income from foreign assets would be negative; and in the case of a borrowing country, the savings lent abroad would be negative. In these cases it might be more convenient to rearrange the table so as to bring positive items on to each side; the foreign borrowing would then appear on the right-hand side, the interest on foreign obligations would appear on the left.

These adjustments would be convenient, but it should be

noticed that if the table was written in this way, the totals to which the columns would add up would no longer be constituent parts of the national income; the foreign borrowing, for example, is clearly not a part of income. This new table is therefore a table of the balance of payments, not exclusively 'on income account.'

Before we can write down a table of the balance of payments in this new sense, one further adjustment is, however, still needed—an adjustment which may be important even in the case of a creditor and lending country. By 'net investment out of imports' we mean the value of goods imported during the year and added to home equipment, *minus* the value of any goods taken from the initial equipment and exported. On the same principle of taking negative items across to the other side of the balance, these exports from initial equipment should be taken across and added to the other exports. When this has been done we shall find that we have got *all* the exports of the year on one side of the balance, and *all* the imports on the other.

The balance of payments equation can therefore be written in the following simple form:

For a creditor-lending country

Imports	= Exports
plus	*plus*
Net foreign lending	Net income from foreign assets

For a debtor-borrowing country

Imports	= Exports
plus	*plus*
Net interest, etc., on foreign liabilities	Net foreign borrowing

The two sides of this equation are *necessarily* equal; the equality between them is absolutely fundamental for the understanding of a nation's international economic position.[5]

[5] For the senses in which the terms 'favorable' and 'adverse' may be applied to the balance of payments, see Appendix, Note D.

4. Monetary Approach to the Balance of Payments Equation

The balance of payments equation can also be arrived at in another way—perhaps an easier way. As we have seen, the money possessed by a particular person (or firm) at a particular time consists of nothing else but a debt to the holder from his bank (or, in the case of bank notes, from the bank which has issued the notes). Therefore, if an English firm buys cotton from the United States, the only way in which the import can be paid for in the first place is by giving the American seller a claim on an English bank; the transferring of this claim may take various forms,[6] but the simplest is to hand over a check. The check is an instruction to the English bank to transfer part of the money which stands to the credit of the English buyer and put it to the credit of the American seller. The result of the transaction is that the English buyer acquires the cotton, and the American seller acquires a claim on the English bank—a debt due to him by the English bank. If the American seller now deposits the check in his own bank in America, the American bank acquires the claim on the English bank, but has a debt owing to the American seller to set on the other side of its account.

There are thus at least four parties to the transaction—the English buyer, the American seller, the English bank, the American bank. The transactions between the English buyer and the English bank, and between the American seller and the American bank, are internal to their respective countries, so they do not affect the balance of payments. As between England and America, there is the English import of American cotton, and the debt from the English bank to the American bank which offsets it. And that is all. England has im-

[6] The other forms (bills of exchange, etc.) are described in all textbooks on money.

ported the cotton, and an English bank has borrowed from an American bank to 'finance' the import.

The same thing happens when anything else is exported from the United States, including security exports and 'invisible' exports of insurance services and the like. All these things involve loans by American banks to banks abroad.

Most of these loans, however, are speedily cancelled out. For when foreign commodities are imported into the United States, or when foreigners receive American dividend checks, or when Americans buy foreign securities or travel abroad, interbank debts are set up which go in the opposite direction. All these dealings involve loans from foreign banks to American banks.

Ordinarily these two sets of bank debts cancel one another out almost completely. If so, the balance of payments equation will still be approximately correct if written without any term for interbank loans. But to get a strict balance which will hold in all conditions, bank lending as well as all other lending across frontiers must be taken into account.

Nevertheless, bank lending or borrowing, necessary to settle differences, is not like other lending or borrowing; when it increases beyond a certain point, trouble arises. For the amounts which the banks of any nation can borrow from the banks of other nations in this way are limited; the limits may vary in different circumstances, but they are always there. If a country is unable to pay for its imports (and for the loans which its citizens are making to foreigners) except by a large amount of such bank borrowing, it is in an awkward position. (This was the position which Great Britain reached in the autumn of 1931, when the gold standard was abandoned.) To extend the study of the balance of payments to cover the means for dealing with such a situation would take us beyond the scope of this book.

5. THE MECHANISM OF INTERNATIONAL LENDING

The balance of payments equation throws a great amount of light upon another range of problems also. When we are concerned with the broad movements of economic history, we need not pay much attention to the balancing loans of the banks, which are only important at moments of crisis. We can write the balance equation in approximate form with only a small error:

Net Foreign lending =
$$\text{Exports} - \text{Imports} + \text{Net Income from foreign assets}$$

and not worry much about the bank lending.

Now consider the position of a country, such as Great Britain must have been at some time in the late eighteenth century, which is neither a creditor nor a debtor country to any considerable extent. If such a country lends abroad, it can only do so by exporting more than it imports. This is the first phase of lending. After it has lent abroad for a number of years, the interest on its past loans will begin to amount to a considerable sum, so that if it is to retain a surplus of exports over imports, it must lend abroad more than ever. This seems to have been the usual situation of Britain after 1850; she was still lending abroad, still adding to her foreign assets; but her new lending was usually rather less than the interest on her old loans, so she had a surplus of imports over exports.

Now suppose that as a result of some emergency, such as a war, the country which had been lending abroad starts to borrow abroad, or to sell off its foreign assets. During the war, since net foreign lending is negative, and net income from foreign assets is still positive, the excess of imports over exports becomes much larger than usual. But this excess of imports is paid for by giving up foreign assets; if the loss of foreign assets is large, net income from foreign assets will be much reduced when the war is over; consequently the country will be unable to lend abroad and build up its foreign assets at the old rate, unless it manages with a smaller excess of imports over exports than it did in the past. Something like this seems to have been the situation of Great Britain between 1919 and 1939; during these years her net foreign lending was very small indeed. It will be observed that if the loss of foreign assets had gone even farther than it did, so that there was no net income from foreign assets any longer, the country would only have been able to lend abroad, and so build up its foreign assets again, if it could secure an excess of exports over imports, as in the first phase.

So far we have considered the position of a lending country, which only borrows in an extraordinary emergency; but for every lender there must be a borrower—where could the normal lending of the earlier phases go to? It is perfectly reasonable and sensible for a country to borrow abroad as a normal policy if the borrowing is used productively—if it enables the borrowing country to make net additions to its national capital. The national capital of a borrowing country, let us remember, consists of the capital equipment it possesses at home *minus* its foreign debts. If foreign borrowing is spent wastefully, it involves a net loss of national capital, just because debts mount up; but if the borrowing is employed to make additions to home equipment, which are more valuable than the debt outstanding against them, then national capital is actually increased as a result of the borrowing. There can be little doubt that most of the foreign borrowing carried out by overseas countries has been of this type; the British Dominions and even the United States could not have grown as they have done if they had not borrowed on a vast scale during their period of growth.

The phases of borrowing can be followed through in the same way as the phases of lending. Suppose that a country (which is initially neither a creditor nor a debtor) begins to borrow abroad; then in the first phase its imports will exceed its exports. The additional imports may consist of capital goods or of consumption goods; it should be noticed that the import of large quantities of consumption goods, financed by borrowing, does not necessarily mean that the borrowing is being used unproductively. For the import of consumption goods may enable the country's own labor force to be turned over to the production of new capital equipment. If the consumption goods had not been imported, they would have to have been produced at home; if they do not need to be produced at home, the factors of production which might have produced them can be used to make additions to equipment. In a practical case, when a country borrows to build a railway, the additional imports consist partly of railway equipment produced abroad, partly of consumption goods supplied to the workers who are installing the equipment or doing the other parts of the construction which have to be done on the spot. Or perhaps the rearrangement of production is even more complicated; but the principle remains the same.

The second phase on the borrowing side comes when the interest on past borrowings mounts up; then (exactly as in the lending case) the country will have to borrow even more rapidly than before if it is to retain a surplus of imports over exports. If the rate of borrowing falls off, or fails to expand, sooner or later a point must be reached when exports must exceed imports. In practice, this point always is reached after a certain time.

If the borrowing has been used productively, the excess of exports over imports can generally be brought about with very little trouble. For the increase in capital equipment will have increased the nation's productive power; the production of goods is increased, and out of this increased production, extra goods can be spared for export without any great sacrifice. We do in fact observe that in the latter years of the nineteenth century, when the second phase was reached by a large number of debtor countries, their exports (particularly their exports of raw materials and foodstuffs) expanded notably. Out of these exports they paid the interest on their debts, but they were able to pay and still to enjoy a mounting prosperity.

Productive lending and borrowing, as we have been describing it, is a profoundly beneficent process. Without the international lending of the nineteenth century, the productive powers of the borrowing countries could hardly have been developed at more than a snail's pace; and without the development of production in new lands the older countries would have lacked the foodstuffs and raw materials which have enabled them to support rising populations at rising standards of living. It is highly probable that the economic opportunities for such productive lending are far from exhausted; the mass of poverty in China and India still needs a vast increase of capital equipment if it is to be remedied, and it is unlikely that the peoples of those countries will be able to provide it from their own savings within any measurable period.

We should never forget, however, that international lending leads to political difficulties which do not arise from internal lending. The fact that borrower and lender live under different governments and different legal systems may make the obligation from borrower to lender harder to enforce; thus international lending will often proceed more smoothly (lenders will be more willing to lend) if the government of the lending country can influence the government of the borrowing country to see that the debts due to its citizens are respected. But such pressure is often resented, and sometimes resisted—even Russian Communism was originally, in one of its aspects, a revolt against the 'tyranny of international capital.' When the citizens of a strong country lend to those of a weaker, international lending may be the forerunner of Imperialism. It is hard to be fair in these matters; but if Imperialism is the bad side of international lending, it may also be claimed that productive lending is one of the good sides of Imperialism.

The great wars of the twentieth century have caused vast dislocations in the international debt structure. War debts are more disturbing than most other debts; they arise so suddenly that industries have no time to be adapted to them, and they are accompanied by no increase of productive power in the debtor countries. The case of Germany in the 1920's is a celebrated example. As a result of the foreign liabilities imposed on her by reparations, and by the interest on loans which she had raised to restore her working capital after the ravages of war and postwar mismanagement, she found herself (by 1928-9) under the necessity of creating a surplus of exports over imports, without having the time or opportunity to reshape her industrial system so as to be able to create that surplus in a tolerable way. The corresponding adjustment in the United States, though in the opposite direction, likewise created difficulties. The natural consequence of America's newly acquired position as a creditor would have been the creation of an import surplus; but her manufacturing interests struggled against any tendency to an increase in imports, her agricultural interests were threatened with ruin by a fall in exports; the balance of payments was inexorable, so an absurd way out (which caused the maximum of inconvenience to the rest of the world) was found by importing first gold, then shaky securities, then gold again. It would have been far better both for America and for other countries if she had taken the opportunity to develop a steady outflow of productive loans. But owing to a mixture of political disturbances, economic misfortunes abroad, and sheer ineptness in selecting borrowers, the American foreign investments built up in 1923-30 involved very heavy losses. Having burned his fingers, the American investor retired into his shell.

6. VISIBLES AND INVISIBLES

Before concluding this chapter, one final remark of some importance needs to be made. I have throughout used the words *imports* and *exports* to mean *all* goods and services sold by members of the nation to outsiders or bought by them from outsiders. This is the natural economic meaning. But before we can apply our reasoning to the published statistics of imports and exports, a warning is necessary. The imports and exports recorded in the statistics are only those which pass under the noses of customs officials at ports or customs houses; but not all the things which are imports or exports in the economic sense do so. The imports and exports which are recorded by the customs officials are called *visible;* the others are called *invisible.* A very important invisible export of Great Britain is the transport by shipping which British sailors perform for outsiders; another is the insurance done for foreigners by British insurance companies; neither of these gets included in the official statistics of exports. Another invisible export is the services performed for foreign tourists. When Americans travel in England, England is (invisibly) exporting; when Englishmen travel on the Continent, England is (invisibly) importing.

XIII

THE STATE AND THE NATIONAL INCOME

1. The Collective Services of Order and Defense

The second set of qualifications to the principle that the sum of incomes equals the net value of output relates to the economic activities of government.

The key functions of government, despite many additions, are still in the field of 'Justice, Police, and Arms' (to use the language of Adam Smith): we need government to protect the community against internal disorder and external aggression. These functions have to be carried on by government officers (soldiers and sailors, policemen, judges, civil servants). These people have to be paid, and equipment and supplies bought for their use; and these expenditures have to be met by taxes (i.e. compulsory contributions levied upon citizens) and by borrowing.

How do these activities fit into our account of the earning and spending of the national income? The usual solution is to say that the work of the government is carried on, like that of industry, to satisfy the wants of the community, and that the taxes and loans which finance government are thus really expenditures of the citizens, just like their purchases of food and clothing. The suggested analogy is that of a voluntary association. When a country club hires men to keep the golf course in order, the work is done for the benefit of members and paid for out of their dues and fees; and there can be no doubt that these dues and fees classify as consumption expenditures. True, the State is a compulsory association, not a voluntary one. People have to pay taxes whether they like it or not, and cannot easily protect themselves against what they consider unjust treatment by joining another club instead. Consequently, fairness in charging shares of the expense to different people is a more critical issue in the State than in the country club. But the existence of this problem does not prevent us from regarding the taxes which pay for public services as analogous to club subscriptions, and public expenditures as expenditures on account of citizens.

2. DIRECT AND INDIRECT PRODUCTIVENESS OF GOVERNMENT

There is, however, a further question. Granted that the services which maintain order and defense are to be regarded as productive (and for lack of a better measure that they are to be valued at cost), they may be:

1. Services which satisfy the wants of consumers directly; or
2. Services which facilitate the production of goods and services by private industry; or
3. Public Investment operations, making concrete additions to the nation's stock of wealth.

How can government services serving these different purposes be segregated?

There are, of course, instances in which classification is easy. If the municipality hires musicians to give a band concert on a summer evening, that is consumption. If a river channel is kept dredged for commercial traffic, that is facilitating production. If a bridge is built, that is public investment. But unfortunately many of the most important activities of government are not so easily classified, particularly as between direct consumption and aid to production: they are partly one and partly the other.

The wicked millionaire, whose well-deserved murder has served as the theme of so many detective stories, often employs a private bodyguard. If we met such a case in real life, we should have no more hesitation in classifying the bodyguard's wages as part of the millionaire's personal expenditure than the wages of the chauffeur and butler who also figure in detective stories. Most of us are contented to satisfy our much more modest wants for personal protection by relying upon the police and other governmental defense forces. Consequently, expenditures on policing (or the taxes which finance them) seem to be a reasonable inclusion in consumption expenditure. On the other hand, consider the case of a firm which (lacking adequate police protection) employs a night-watchman to keep its goods from being stolen. His wages are clearly part of the cost of the firm's output; his services are embodied in the output which they help to produce, not a net addition to social product over and above that output. If now the city adds the former night-watchman to its police force, levying taxes on business to cover his pay, and gives the firm police protection which is thorough enough to make it useless to hire another watchman, it is plain that the police services in question contribute to social output in exactly the same way. Police protection for a warehouse district is not unproductive; but its fruits are embodied in the output of industry just like the fruits of the services of the private watchman. When we remember that the policemen in the warehouse districts have the incidental job of keeping tipsy night-wanderers from falling into the river, those in residential districts also protect property—while one chief of police supervises both—it is plain that there is no easy way to say how much of the cost of police work is directed towards protecting life, liberty, and personal safety, and how much towards protecting the productive process.

Similar difficulties apply to the classification of most other lines of government activity. Consequently national income statisticians lack a satisfactory basis for allocating government services among the three classes. So far as possible, they try to present material so as to make such an allocation unnecessary.

3. Allocation of Factor Costs to Government

For most purposes, it is useful to measure the parts of the social output 'at factor cost'—i.e. to value each part according to the amount paid for the services of persons and property used in producing it. If we could classify government services on the system given above, it would be interesting to allocate factor costs to consumption *including* government services which lead to direct consumption or facilitate the current flow of finished goods, and investment *including* public investment and government services which facilitate private investment. This cannot be done satisfactorily. But it is reasonably satisfactory to allocate factor costs under three headings—consumption of products of industry; investment carried on by industry; and government. On this basis, the factor cost of government is the sum of the personal incomes actually arising in government (chiefly the salaries of government employees [1]) *plus* the factor cost of the products of industry consumed in government operations (stationery, fuel, arms, etc.). The factor cost of consumption and private investment is the amount of personal incomes arising in private industry *less* the factor cost of the products of industry consumed in government. For the purpose of gauging the possibilities of shifting national resources from one use to another, this classification would be improved very little by trying to distinguish between directly productive government services and those indirectly productive.

4. Difficulty of Measuring Government Contribution to Economic Welfare

One major use of national income calculations, however, is poorly served by this rough classification—namely, the meas-

[1] For reasons which will appear shortly, interest on the debts of local government is included among factor costs, while interest on the debt of the central government is excluded.

urement of changes in economic welfare. For reasons developed in later chapters,[2] consumption of goods and services produced by private industry should be measured for this purpose at the market prices actually paid by consumers, which exceed factor costs by the amount of indirect taxes [3] which are paid through consumption expenditure. Private investment also is best measured at market prices. If the market prices of all goods and services bought by government are added on, the total will exceed national income (which is the sum of all factor costs) by the total amount of indirect taxes paid. Another way of putting this is that national income will exceed private consumption and investment by the excess of government expenditure on goods and services over government receipts from indirect taxes. Statistically, the result is the same as if the indirect taxes were taken to measure the indirectly productive services of government—those which facilitate production in private industry, rather than constitute public investment or social consumption. Actually, of course, there is no reason to suppose that indirect taxes change from time to time in the same direction as government services aimed to facilitate production, let alone by the same amount. A rise of social consumption through better parks, for instance, might be financed by a sales tax or heavier property taxes; or a reduction of services which facilitate production could lead to a reduction of income taxes (which are 'direct' rather than 'indirect') or of government borrowing. Consequently the excess of national income over the value at market prices of private consumption and investment is not a good measure of social consumption and investment; and this inaccuracy limits the usefulness of estimates based on market prices.

[2] Chs. xv, xvi, below. See also Appendix, Note E, pp. 250 ff.

[3] Taxes paid on sales or imports of commodities, plus state and local general property taxes. They are 'indirect' in that the tax payment passes from the consumer regarded as taxpayer to the tax collector through an intermediary—taxes on owner-occupied property (sometimes classified as 'direct' for this reason) being an exception.

5. THE SPECIAL PROBLEM OF WAR; THE NATIONAL DEBT

A peculiarly difficult problem in the relation of government to the national income accounts is presented by war. As more and more resources go into war production, private consumption and investment fall far short of national income. Thus in 1943, with a national income (according to the definition of this book) of about $165 billion, the United States had at market prices consumption of $93 billion and net private dis-investment [3a] of about $8 billion, leaving a difference of about $80 billion; at factor costs, allowing for indirect taxes of over $12 billion, the difference was over $90 billion, or considerably more than consumption at factor costs.

To regard this excess as social consumption might conceivably make sense for an aggressor nation, on the theory that war is analogous to the provision of a free circus on a gigantic scale. But for a nation which accepts war only as a necessary evil, it is impossible to accept this as a true account of the facts. Clearly, war cannot be regarded as primarily public investment in the sense of building up a permanent increase of assets: while there is always some social salvage value in the goods produced during a war, it is only a fraction of the total, and must be regarded as merely a by-product. It might be more sensible to regard war activity as investment in an intangible asset called Freedom; but neither the money value nor the necessary postwar amortization of such an asset can be determined statistically, and, in general, investment in intangibles is not recognized in income accounting.

To treat war activity as contributing neither to investment

[3a] That is, depreciation and similar charges on privately owned capital (amounting to about $10 billion) plus using up of inventories (about $1 billion), plus accumulation of debts to foreign countries (about $2 billion) outweighed the roughly $5 billion worth of new buildings and equipment going into private ownership. Most of the new ships, factories, etc., built in 1943 went into government ownership and thus did not count in the product of private industry.

nor to consumption would result in a total product far below the value of incomes received by citizens; for of course war work leads to wages, profits, etc., like any other work. Thus this treatment would involve writing a large negative adjustment item labelled 'social war losses' at the bottom of the national income table to balance the account. On the whole, it seems more satisfactory to stick to the valuation procedure which makes the product come out equal to the income, with suitable mental reservations. Since government appears as a separate component in the product account, the student is not likely to confuse it either with private consumption or private investment.

So long as war is not treated as investment, a necessary corrolary is the treatment of interest on the national debt which has become standard in British (but not in American) official estimates. If the war is charged off currently as it goes on, the war debt must be regarded as a 'dead-weight debt,' like the debt of the spendthrift heir discussed in Chapter x above. In the case of the spendthrift, it is possible to regard the interest as part of his creditor's income without double-counting, so long as we charge the interest as a business expense to the spendthrift (which means subtracting it from his income). But parallel treatment for the national debt would require regarding the part of taxes paid to carry debt interest as not part of the taxpayers' income, which is simply not the way taxpayers' incomes are thought of. Consequently consistency requires subtracting the amount of interest on the federal [4] debt

---

[4] It is customary, however, to regard interest on state and local government debts as a payment for productive services—namely the services of the schools, highways, parks, public buildings, waterworks, etc., to which such debts normally correspond. If war were capitalized as an intangible durable asset, it might make sense also to treat interest on the war debt in similar fashion. But it must be remembered that upkeep and depreciation on the schools, etc., are provided for. In the case of a war debt, if the benefit of winning the war were assumed to wear off in a generation or so, the interest even at the outset would not much

from the aggregate of individual incomes in obtaining national income.

6. The Socialized Industries

We must now turn to the other functions of government, which are not related to the central functions of law, order, and defense. In the first place, we have the socialized industries. The scope of socialization varies a great deal between one country and another, the reasons being partly 'ideological,' partly mere convenience. There is a tendency for the industries which are selected for socialization to belong to a distinctive group. The post office is socialized everywhere; many countries (though not the United States or Britain) have socialized railways; then there are the so-called 'public utility' industries of water, gas, local transit, and electricity. As regards these latter, British and American practice differs from place to place; the public-utility undertakings operating in a particular district are sometimes owned by the local authority, sometimes not. It is an interesting question why these industries should have a particular tendency to be socialized—or, if not actually socialized, to be brought under particularly stringent state control—but we cannot go into that question here.

The socialized industries fit into our scheme of the national income without any difficulty; we treat them just as we treat other industries. Like the products of other industries, the products of the socialized industries are sold; the receipts from these sales go to cover costs in the usual way, and to pay interest on the capital employed. Since it is always possible for a deficit in the running of a public undertaking to be met

exceed the depreciation; and after a few years it would be much less. Such a system of accounting would definitely imply charging part of the cost of war against peace-time years, and thus on the whole reducing rather than increasing the income of those years as compared with estimates made on the system of the text above. Cf. Simon Kuznets, *National Product in Wartime*, New York, 1945.

out of taxes, the whole of the capital needed for it can be raised by borrowing; there are no ordinary shares. A public undertaking can therefore raise its capital a little more cheaply than a private firm can do; but this does not necessarily mean that it will produce more cheaply, for it is only too easy to throw away such an advantage by using larger amounts of the factors of production per unit of output.

There is one important socialized industry which is in a different category. The provision of roads is nearly always socialized, this time for a very obvious reason. Private enterprise could only charge for the use of a road by imposing tolls, and toll-gates are an intolerable nuisance. For the same reason, the public authority cannot charge for the use of roads directly, but must finance its expenditure on roads out of taxation. We must, therefore, regard roads as a public service in the same class as order and defense. The same problem arises over roads as arose over those other public services: are they consumption goods in their own right, or do they assist in the production of other consumption goods? Once again the answer must be that they are partly one, partly the other; but once again there is no means of distinguishing between private and commercial uses, so we have to write down the whole of the upkeep of roads as a form of consumption expenditure, for which the government acts as agent. The construction of new roads, on the other hand, is clearly investment; when the government finances the building of new roads out of taxation (as it has usually done) it imposes upon the community a form of compulsory saving.

7. SOCIAL SERVICES AND TRANSFER EXPENDITURE

Most of the remaining functions of government are what is known as 'social' in character. The function of Poor Relief was first taken over by the State from the Church at the time of the Reformation; but partly as the result of the growth of a social conscience, partly because of the increasing political

power of the beneficiaries, the things done by the State with
the direct object of improving the position of the less well-to-
do have increased enormously during the last hundred years,
and particularly within the present century. Public health,
education, and unemployment relief are major items in the
expenditure of local authorities; the central government shares
in these, and aids expenditure on housing and old-age pensions. The 'social' element in British public expenditure was
at its highest, relative to other elements, in the early 1930's,
when it was swollen by the abnormal unemployment and
when military expenditure had not yet begun to rise in preparation for the storm which broke in 1939. Thus in the year
1934, central and local authorities together were spending
almost exactly £1,000 millions [5] which had to be covered out
of taxes, and nearly half of it was social expenditure. In the
United States, on the other hand, where social expenditure was
less developed, there was an increase through the 1930's; federal expenditure for these purposes rising from about $2 bil-
lion in the 1933-4 fiscal year to about $3 billion in 1938-9. For
the fiscal year 1937-8 (a representative year for which records
on a comparable basis for federal, state, and local governments have been assembled), about one-third of the $17½ bil-
lion in their combined budgets was for social purposes. Not
by any means the whole of this social expenditure should be
regarded as money taken from the relatively wealthy and
used for the advantage of the less wealthy; all classes make
some contribution to taxes, and a considerable part of the
social expenditure is distributed through insurance schemes,
to which the same people who benefit when they are in need
make contributions when they can afford it.[6] Yet whatever

[5] The £200 millions spent on operating socialized industries, recovered
by selling the products of those industries, is not included. For further
details, see U. K. Hicks, *The Finance of British Government*, ch. 2.

[6] The cynical comment on these insurance schemes is that they are a
means of making it look as if there is more social expenditure for the
benefit of the less wealthy than there really is; on the other hand, it

allowance we make for these contributions, the fact remains that 'social' activities are now a major part of the functions of government.

'Social' expenditure has a very different social and political significance from that of the other functions of government which we have been discussing; but when we come to fitting it into our account of the national income, we find that it will go into the old compartments, though it has to be divided between the compartments. When the State employs teachers or doctors, it is organizing a service for the community in the same way as when it employs policemen or soldiers; if some members of the community do not take advantage of the public health or education services, but prefer to satisfy their own wants in another way, that makes no more difference to the classification than was made by our millionaire's bodyguard. A large part of social expenditure is thus to be regarded as expenditure on public services, in the way with which we are already familiar.

There is, however, another part of social expenditure which is not spent directly on public services, but is handed over to the beneficiaries for them to spend themselves. Old-age pensions and most unemployment assistance are of this type. Now if we regard these cash benefits and pensions as income of the recipients, we must not also regard the money which is spent on them as part of the incomes of the taxpayers or contributors from whom it is collected. It does not matter very much whose income we reckon it to be, so long as we do not count it twice. If we like, we can say that the government takes away a part of the incomes of the contributors and transfers it to the pensioners; if so, we count the pensions as true incomes of the pensioners, while the true incomes of the contributors are less than their nominal incomes. Or perhaps it is

may be argued that the insurance device has a real social advantage, for it enables the beneficiary to receive his benefits as a right, and not as 'charity.'

better to say that the contributors are compelled to save some parts of their incomes and to pay them into a pension fund, while the government borrows these savings and transfers them to the pensioners, who are thus enabled to spend in excess of their true incomes.[7] In either case, we have a distinction between true income and nominal income, just as we had in the case of the national debt. *Transfers* due to either cause have got to be deducted from the total of nominal incomes before the national income is arrived at.

[7] This latter way of putting it is distinctly more convenient in cases (such as that of Britain in 1931) when the government's payments in unemployment relief are in excess of the contributions and tax receipts available to finance them, so that special borrowing is necessary. The same approach is also convenient for dealing with such questions as that of old-age retirement funds. It should be noticed that if a person saves part of his income in one year, and spends these savings in the next year, he is spending in excess of his income in the second year.

XIV

THE NATIONAL INCOME OF THE
UNITED STATES IN 1939

1. THE 1939 BASE DATE

We have now reached a point where it will be useful to look at some concrete figures, so as to see how the calculation of the national income comes out in a particular case—that of the United States in 1939.

As was stated above, estimates can be made both from the income side and from the output side. Income estimates have been the object of continuous study at the National Bureau of Economic Research since the end of the First World War; and the United States Department of Commerce has been making official estimates since 1934 which represent a development of this pioneer work.

Output estimates have only been filled out in the important service sector in very recent years. The output estimates, as was noted above, are a mixture of expenditure data on the consumption side and commodity-flow data on the investment side. Like the income estimates, they have been developed by the Department of Commerce largely on the basis of pioneer work done privately—chiefly at the National Bureau.

The selection of 1939 as the most useful single year to study rests on several considerations. The year 1939 is at once the terminal year of the interwar period (World War II having taken strong hold on the American economy by 1940), the last year for which a full array of census data is available, and the year of greatest production prior to World War II. It has served as base for most analyses of the war economy, and will doubtless long serve—as did 1913 for decades—as the standard prewar year for comparisons of postwar with prewar conditions.

2. Income Payments to Individuals

To begin with the income side, 'income payments to individuals' amounted in 1939 to $70.8 billion, made up as follows:

	Billions	*Billions*
Wages and salaries	$43.8	
Work relief wages	1.9	
Direct and other relief	1.1	
Social security benefits	0.9	
Other compensation of employees	0.8	
Total compensation of employees, cash basis		$48.5
Profits of farmers	$4.3	
Profits of other self-employed business and professional men	6.9	
Total income of self-employed		$11.2
Dividends	$3.8	
Interest, including federal debt	5.1	
Net cash rents and mine and patent royalties	2.3	
Income from property, cash basis		$11.2
Rounding errors in figures quoted		−0.1
Total income payments		$70.8

It will be observed that the $48.5 billion of labor income paid to employees makes up 68 per cent of the total; while the $11.2 billion paid to property makes up 16 per cent. A second 16 per cent is accounted for by the incomes of the self-employed, which is a mixture of labor and property income. Since most of the mixture must be attributed to the actual work done by farmers, shopkeepers, and professional men rather than to their property, the total share of property in the income payments must be placed in the neighborhood of 20 per cent—probably less rather than more.

All figures in billions	Income pay-ments	Adjustments to national income basis		National income	
		Subtrac-tions: 'trans-fer pay-ments'	Addi-tions: 'non-cash income'	Amount	Per cent
Wages and salaries:					
Cash	$43.8	....	....	$43.8	60.6
Non-cash	.....	....	$0.4	0.4	0.5
Total	$43.8	....	$0.4	$44.2	61.1
Work relief	1.9	....	....	1.9	2.6
Other relief	1.1	$1.1	....	0.0	0.0
Social security benefits	0.9	0.9	....	0.0	0.0
Employers' contributions to social security funds	.....	....	1.3	1.3	1.8
Other employee compen-sation	0.8	0.1	....	0.7	1.0
Pure labor income	$48.5	$2.1	$1.7	$48.1	66.5
Profits of farmers	$4.3	....	....	$4.3	6.0
Profits of other self-em-ployed	6.9	....	....	6.9	9.5
Mixed labor and prop-erty income	$11.2	....	....	$11.2	15.5
Dividends	$3.8	....	....	$3.8	5.3
Net savings of corpora-tions (i.e. excess of prof-its over dividends)	.....	....	$0.4	$0.4	.6
Funds set aside to pay tax-es on corporate profits	.....	....	1.4	1.4	1.9
Interest and cash rents	7.4	....	....	.....	....
Federal debt interest	.....	$1.0	....	6.4	8.8
Net rental value of owner-occupied homes	.....	....	1.5	1.5	2.1
Less: profits resulting from rising prices on goods in inventory	.....	0.4	....	−0.4	−0.6
Pure property income	$11.2	$1.4	$3.3	$13.1	18.1
Rounding errors	−$0.1	−$0.1	−$0.1	−$0.1	−0.1
National total	$70.8	$3.4	$4.9	$72.3	100.0
Total of nominal incomes*				$74.8	103.5

* Including transfer payments other than Social Security benefits

3. Relation of Income Payments to National Income

The total of income payments differs somewhat from national income: each total includes some items which are excluded from the other. Under the definition of national income used in this book, the necessary adjustments run as shown on page 188. The adjustments for 1939 make national income come out somewhat larger than income payments, and with a somewhat larger proportion (18 per cent instead of 16 per cent) of property income. For postwar years, however, the much larger figure for federal debt interest will bring the national income total below that for income payments.

4. How Individuals Used Their Incomes

How were these incomes used? The sum of all nominal incomes (including the 'transfer payments' subtracted out above, with the exception of social-security benefits, besides national income proper) can be traced either to consumer spending, payment of direct taxes, or savings. The main items (dollar amounts in billions) are given on page 190. The extra 3.5 per cent represents the excess of nominal incomes over national income resulting from the inclusion of $2.5 billion of transfer payments in the former.

5. The Ultimate Spending of the National Income: Allocation of Factor Costs

How were the nation's productive resources allocated among the different lines of production? The answer to this question involves us in the problem of accounting for government activities, which we examined in Chapter xiii. For the values *in market prices* which represent what is actually paid for, the goods and services which make up social output include not only payments for the use of productive resources but also payments of 'indirect' taxes to the government. These taxes, as we saw in Chapter xiii, have next to no relation to

	Amount in billions	% national income
Purchase of 'durable' consumption goods (lasting over 2 yrs.):		
Automobiles and parts	$2.3	3.2
Furniture, etc.	3.0	4.1
Other durable consumption goods	1.1	1.5
	$6.4	8.8
Purchase of 'semi-durable' and perishable consumption goods:		
Clothing, etc.	$6.8	9.4
Motor fuel, etc.	2.1	2.9
Food	18.1	25.0
Tobacco	1.8	2.5
Other consumption goods	3.8	5.3
	$32.6	45.1
Services:		
Cash purchases, including rental of tenant-occupied homes	$22.7	31.4
Rental value of owner-occupied homes	1.5	2.1
Taxes on owner-occupied homes	1.1	1.5
Licenses for pleasure automobiles	0.2	0.3
	$25.5	35.3
Total consumption	$64.5	89.2
Direct taxes:		
Corporate income	$1.4	1.9
Individual income	1.1	1.5
Estate and gift	.5	.7
Poll and personal property taxes	.2	.3
	$3.2	4.4
Savings:		
Net corporate savings minus inventory revaluation correction	$0.0	0.0
Excess of employer plus employee contributions to Social Security over benefits	1.1	1.5
Other net savings of individuals	6.0	8.3
	$7.1	9.8
Error from rounding figures	0.0	0.1
Total accounted for	$74.8	103.5
Excess of nominal incomes over national income *	$2.5	3.5

* Amount of transfer payments, excluding Social Security benefits because these are ccounted for in putting savings on a net basis.

government services which contribute to making the product in question. To take an extreme case, consumer expenditures for tobacco in 1939 amounted to 2.5 per cent of national income. But nearly two-fifths of this expenditure went to pay for the little blue tax stamps which appear on packages of cigarettes, pipe tobacco, etc. Tobacco accounted for only about 1.5 per cent of the social product at factor cost—i.e. for only 1.5 per cent of the actual payments for the use of productive resources. If consumers had elected to give up tobacco, and its production had stopped completely, 2.5 per cent could have been added to expenditure on other things without any change in money incomes; but only 1.5 per cent could have been added to the *production* of other things by re-employing the labor, land, etc., no longer used for tobacco.[1]

To allocate factor costs, it is necessary to start by valuing the various parts of the national product at market prices and then subtract the estimated indirect taxes included in the price of each component. This calculation is shown on page 192. These figures show that three-quarters of the nation's resources in use in 1939 were used for consumption. The 4 per cent going into investment was very small in comparison. The 20 per cent going into government was substantial relative to consumption. An invention permitting the work of government to be done with half the 1939 manpower would have permitted a transfer of 10 per cent of the nation's resources— capable of increasing consumption by about ⅐th. By way of perspective, unemployment in 1940 (which was a year of somewhat larger production than 1939) was about ⅕th as large as employment, as was shown in Chapter VI; and there was also probably some 'concealed unemployment.' Possibili-

[1] While factor cost is a better measure than market price of the resources employed, it remains an unsatisfactory measure. Even factor cost fails to allow for the effect of monopolistic arrangements in pushing resources out of their most efficient uses, and for the fact that some highly specialized resources would be less productive if used in different ways than they now are.

Component	Value at market prices		Indirect taxes (billions)	Value at factor cost	
	Per cent	Amount (billions)		Amount (billions)	Per cent
Consumption					
Durable commodities	7.7	$6.4	$0.5	$5.9	8.2
Other consumers' commodities	39.4	32.6	5.1	27.5	38.0
Consumption services	30.8	25.5	4.3	21.2	29.3
Total consumption	77.9	$64.5	$9.9	$54.6	75.5
Investment:					
Residential construction	2.4	$2.0	.....	.....	.....
Other construction	1.9	1.6	.....	.....	.....
Producers' durable equipment (machinery etc.)	6.6	5.5	.....	.....	.....
Net growth in business inventories	1.1	0.9	.....	.....	.....
Net exports of goods and services	1.0	0.8	.....	.....	.....
Net exports and monetary use of gold and silver	0.2	0.2	.....	.....	.....
'Gross private capital formation'	13.2	$10.9	$0.8	$10.1	14.0
Less depreciation, etc.	−9.4	−7.8	−0.6	−7.2	−10.0
Total investment (net)	3.8	$3.1	$0.2	$2.9	4.0
Government:					
Direct productive services	10.9	$9.0	$0.0	$9.0	12.5
Commodities and services bought from industry	7.2	6.0	0.4	5.6	7.7
Total government	18.1	$15.0	$0.4	$14.6	20.2
Error from rounding figures	.2	$0.2	0.0	$0.2	0.3
Total	100.0	$82.8	$10.5	$72.3	100.0

ties of increasing consumption by fuller use of idle resources were thus much larger than practical possibilities in the direction of transferring resources from government or investment activity.

6. COMPARISON OF DIFFERENT ALLOCATIONS OF INCOME

These four ways of breaking down the total of national income are shown comparatively in Table VI, which includes also for good measure a breakdown by the industry in which income is earned. In the first two columns of the table, we examine the cash receipts of individuals, adjusting them to allow for receipts which are not part of national income (excluding transfers and subtracting out federal-debt interest), and to allow for elements of income which are not cash receipts (adding the rental value of owner-occupied homes and those parts of corporate profits which are not paid out to individuals). In the third column, the incomes are divided up as the receivers dispose of them, with adjustments for direct taxes and for the effect of transfers and public-debt interest. In the fourth and fifth columns, the consumption component of Column C recurs. But instead of direct taxes and savings, the rest of the product is accounted for by investment and government activity.

Comparing columns E and C, it will be observed that in 1939 the $3.1 billion of investment fell considerably short of the $7.1 billion of savings. On the other hand, government took in $10.5 billion of indirect taxes and $3.2 billion of direct taxes—a total of $13.7 billion—while spending $15.0 billion for goods and services and $2.4 billion for transfers. The part of the savings not absorbed by investment went directly and indirectly to finance the resulting governmental deficit. For years with a surplus of government revenues over expenditures, investment will be found to exceed savings by the amount of the surplus.

Table VI

National Income of United States, 1939 (000,000,000 omitted)

A. Income by industry		B. Income by type		C. Disposal of income		D. Product at factor cost		E. Product at market prices	
Agriculture	$5.2	Wages and salaries	$44.2	Consumption	$64.5	Consumption	$54.6	Consumption	$64.5
Mining	1.4	Supplements	3.9	Direct taxes	3.2	Investment	2.9	Investment	3.1
Manufacturing	17.0			Savings	7.1	Government	14.6	Government	15.0
Contract construction	1.9	Employee compensation	$48.1					Adjustment for rounding error	.2
Material goods	$25.5	Profits of:		Subtotal	$74.8	Subtotal	$72.1		
		Farmers	$4.3	Adjustments:		Adjustment for rounding error	$0.2	Subtotal	$82.8
Trade	$11.0	Other self-employed	6.9	Federal debt interest	—$1.0			Less indirect taxes	10.5
Transportation	4.9			Other transfers excluding Social Security	—1.5				
Communication	.9	Mixed labor and property incomes	$11.2		—$2.5				
Distributive trades	$16.8								
Service trades	$7.0	Property incomes	$13.1						
Power and gas	1.5	Adjustment for rounding error	—$0.1						
Finance and real estate	8.3								
Miscellaneous	3.2								
Services	$20.0								
Government:									
Federal	$5.2								
State and local	4.8								
	$10.0								
Adjustments:									
Funds to meet corporate taxes	$1.4								
Federal debt interest	—1.0								
Inventory revaluation	—0.4								
	$0.0								
National income	$72.3	National income	$72.3	National income	$72.3	Net social product	$72.3	Net social product	$72.3

7. SHARES OF PERSONAL SERVICES AND OF PROPERTY

It was indicated above that nearly 80 per cent of the national income of 1939 represented payment for personal exertion and rather over 20 per cent payment for use of property. It would be interesting to break down the three right-hand columns of Table VI to show separately the division of expenditure and disposal over the national product for each of these two broad types of income. Such a breakdown has been undertaken for the British national income of 1938 in the English edition of this book; but American data will not bear the weight of a parallel calculation. We may be rather confident, however, that property income carried in 1939 the great bulk of the direct taxes. Of the three main items composing these taxes (corporate profits taxes $1.4 billion; estate and gift taxes $0.5 billion; personal income taxes $1.1 billion), the first two by their nature must be regarded as falling on property income. The personal income tax was of course largely on earnings; but since it was paid chiefly by the richest 1 per cent of the population, whose income is made up much more largely of property income than that of the total population, more than one-fifth must be ascribed to property—making not less than $2.2 out of the $3.2 billion of personal taxes. On the other hand, the transfer item of national debt interest flows to property-owners. For 1939, therefore, public finance did not much reduce the property share in the national income. Before allowance for public finance, property income (including a share of the mixed incomes) may be put roughly at $16 billion and income from personal exertion at $56 billion. Subtracting the $3.2 billion of direct taxes and adding $2.5 billion for transfer payments other than Social Security benefits, shares in disposable income may be placed at $15 billion for property and $57 billion for personal exertion plus relief, etc. Since the property income is received almost entirely by persons who also have personal earnings, an allocation of personal savings would be highly arbitrary; but under American conditions in 1939 it would not be reasonable to assume the proportion of disposable income saved to be less for property than for earned income. It follows that consumption probably went to labor in somewhat higher proportion than did income. This conclusion would hold either at market prices or at factor costs; though since such items as domestic service, hotels, and travel were tax-free in 1939 it is likely that the high-income persons receiving the bulk of property income had a slightly higher share of consumption at factor cost than at market prices.

8. RELATION TO FOREIGN PAYMENTS

The effect of international relations on the accounts is much less significant than the effect of government. Net income from foreign assets (over and above interest and dividend payments due foreigners on their holdings of American assets) was less than 5 per cent of property income and less than 1 per cent of national income. Thus the net output allowing for international relations was just perceptibly less than the total national output.

On commodity account, the United States in 1939 exported $3.1 billion worth and imported $2.3 billion worth, with a 'favorable' balance of $0.8 billion. There were considerable 'invisible' imports in the form of tourist expenditures abroad, immigrant remittances, ocean freights, etc.; but also considerable 'invisible' exports in the form of interest and dividends on foreign investments, etc., so that the current account remained strongly 'favorable,' including invisible items. On capital account, there was a net shift of funds to the United States amounting to $1.2 billion. These were the chief factors [2] in

---

[2] For 1939 there is a very large unexplained 'residual' in the United States balance of payments, which may represent in large part capital transactions not picked up by the reporting machinery.

a net movement of $3.1 billion of gold and silver towards the United States.

The excess of merchandise exports is reflected in the item so labelled, amounting to $0.8 billion, in the capital formation account. The $3.1 billion net import of gold and silver, however, is offset against the $3.3 billion increase in the monetary stock of those metals, leaving only $0.2 billion for the capital formation account. This $0.2 billion is part of the national product. But since the exported goods which accounted for the $0.8 billion export surplus are already entered, while the remainder of the increase in the gold stock reflects transactions in pre-existing assets or simply in debts, the import of gold as such does not enter the accounts.

XV

THE NATIONAL INCOME IN REAL
TERMS—INDEX-NUMBERS

1. The Problem of Correcting for Price Changes

The national income consists of a collection of goods and services, reduced to a common basis by being measured in terms of money. We have to use the money measure, because there is no other way in which a miscellaneous collection of different articles can be added together; but when we are seeking to compare the production (or the consumption) of one year with that of another, the use of the money measure may lead us into difficulties. A change in the money value of the national income may be due to a real change in the amounts of goods and services at the disposal of the community; but it may be due to nothing more than a change in prices. If exactly the same quantities of goods were produced in one year as had been produced in another, but in the second year prices were all 25 per cent higher, the money value of the national output would be increased by 25 per cent—but this increase would have a different significance from that of an actual increase of 25 per cent in the production of goods and services. An increase of 25 per cent in the *real* output of goods and services would be an economic gain of tremendous significance; an increase of 25 per cent in money values, without any increase in real output, would not represent any economic gain at all. Before we can proceed with our discussions, we must learn something about the means which are available for separating these two sorts of changes from one another.

It must be emphasized, in the first place, that no perfectly satisfactory method of separation exists. If a change in prices meant a change of all prices in the same proportion, it would be easy to correct for the change in prices; we should simply adjust all prices by the same uniform percentage, and we should then be able to proceed as if no change in prices had occurred. Alternatively, if when the output of goods increased or diminished, the outputs of all goods and services increased or diminished in the same proportion, it would then be perfectly clear what the percentage change in real output had been; we should find it easy to avoid being entangled in changes of prices. In practice, these conveniently simple cases never occur. Between one year and another the outputs of some goods increase, those of others diminish; the prices of some goods increase, those of others decrease; even if (as sometimes happens) the prices of nearly all goods increase together, or diminish together, they increase or diminish by very different percentages. We are therefore reduced to make-shifts. It is a very delicate matter (which lies far outside the scope of this book) to distinguish the respective merits of the different makeshifts which are commonly used. Here we can do no more than indicate their general character.

2. The Principle of the Correction

The simplest way of estimating the *real* change in output which takes place from one year to another is to take the different quantities of goods and services produced in the two years and to value each year's quantities at the *same* set of prices. The value of the output of 1930 is ordinarily got by valuing the goods produced in 1930 at the average prices ruling in 1930; the value of the output of 1931 is got by valuing the goods produced in 1931 at the prices of 1931. If we compare these *money* values, we are confronted with a change which is partly due to real changes in output, partly due to changes in prices; but if we use the 1930 prices throughout,

the relation between the figures we shall then get will cease
to be influenced by changes in prices, but will only reflect the
changes in the quantities produced.

For the years 1930 and 1931

$$\text{Ratio between money values of output} = \frac{(\text{Quantities } 1931 \times \text{Prices } 1931)}{(\text{Quantities } 1930 \times \text{Prices } 1930)}$$

$$\text{Ratio between real values of output} = \frac{(\text{Quantities } 1931 \times \text{Prices } 1930)}{(\text{Quantities } 1930 \times \text{Prices } 1930)}$$

The brackets mean that the quantity of each good produced
is to be multiplied by the average price of that good during
the year stated; and the values thus arrived at for the outputs
of different goods are to be added together.

The formula thus given for the ratio between the real
values is got by using the *prices* of 1930 in both the top and
the bottom of the fraction; but there is no particular reason
why we should have selected 1930 as our *base* (as it is called)
rather than some other year; the important thing is that the
prices (but not the quantities) should be the *same* in both
top and bottom. If, instead of valuing both top and bottom
at the prices of 1930, we had valued both at the prices of
1931, we should have got a different formula for the ratio between the real values; there is no obvious reason why one of
these formulae should be better than the other. Fortunately,
in nearly all cases where an experiment has been made, it is
found that the two formulae do not differ very seriously.[1]
Either can therefore be used as a measure of the change in
real value; it does not matter very much which we use.

It is even permissible, provided sufficient care is taken, to
use for valuation the prices of some third year, which is different from either of the two years being compared. Thus it
may be convenient, when we want to trace the movement of
the real national income over a period of years, to select some

[1] There are mathematical reasons why this should be so (cf. Bowley,
Elements of Statistics, pp. 87-8).

particular year as base, and to keep it as base throughout the whole of the calculation. When calculating the movement of the real national income between 1920 and 1940, we might select 1930 as base, and use the prices of 1930 for valuing all the goods and services produced in any of the twenty years. This sort of thing is often done, and there may be no harm in it; but it is rather dangerous. A great deal can happen in twenty years; the circumstances of one year may differ so considerably from those of another year ten years later that the different measures of real income, which would be got by selecting different years (out of the set of twenty years) as bases, might easily differ very considerably. It would be obviously absurd (to take an extreme case) if we tried to compare the real national income of England in 1700 with that in 1800 by using the prices of 1900 as a basis of valuation; indeed it is doubtful if there is any basis of valuation which would enable us to make a useful comparison between the real incomes of two years a century apart. Comparisons of the kind we are discussing are sound and sensible if the circumstances of the two years we are comparing and the circumstances of the base year are not too dissimilar; but when there has been a great change in circumstances, as may sometimes happen even with years which are close together (1939 and 1942 may be a case in point), any kind of comparison needs to be made with great circumspection.

The use of prices just described has the effect of putting different physical units in perspective: prices show, for example, that one small automobile added to production should be viewed as increasing it more than would a hundred pairs of shoes. Consumers are almost always in the position of having the prices of goods set beyond their power to alter, and then deciding how much of each article to buy, within the limits of their incomes. As among the things a given consumer is buying at a given time, the relative prices show the relative importance he places upon having one unit more or less of each. This gives a rough test of the 'similarity' between years which permits real income comparisons: the general structure of ratios between the prices of the main articles of consumption should be unchanged.

3. INDEX-NUMBERS OF PRICES

This is the principle of the method which is used for comparing real income and real output between different years. Even in principle, the method is rather a makeshift; in practice we cannot do even so well as this, at least as a general rule. For although we can acquire, in one way or another, the information which is necessary for calculating the national income valued at the prices of its own year, we do not usually possess the detailed information about the prices and quantities produced of different articles separately, which would be necessary in order to calculate the value of one year's output at the prices of another year. So we are obliged to have recourse to indirect methods. The principle of these indirect methods is the following.

Take the formulae for the ratios of money values of output and of real values of output (between 1930 and 1931) which were set out on a previous page and divide one by the other. The denominators of both fractions are the same and so they cancel out. Thus we get:

$$\frac{\text{Ratio between money values}}{\text{Ratio between real values}} = \frac{(\text{Quantities 1931} \times \text{Prices 1931})}{(\text{Quantities 1931} \times \text{Prices 1930})}$$

The fraction on the right of this new equation has the same *quantities* top and bottom, but different *prices*. It is therefore a measure of the ratio between the levels of *prices* in 1930 and 1931. So we may write:

$$\text{Ratio between real values} = \frac{\text{Ratio between money values}}{\text{Ratio between price levels}}$$

If we can find a way of measuring the ratio between the price levels, the ratio between the real values can be easily calculated from this last formula.

A really satisfactory measure of the ratio between the price levels would of course involve just that knowledge of actual quantities produced, and actual selling prices, which we do not possess. But a rough measure can be reached in other ways. What we need is a measure of the average change in prices which has taken place between the two years. Such measures are called index-numbers.

Index-numbers of prices are put together in what is substantially the following way. We take a particular collection (or 'basket') of goods, so many loaves of bread, so many pounds of sugar, so many pairs of socks, so many ounces of tobacco (and so on);[2] we inquire how much it would have cost to purchase this basket of goods in the year chosen as base, and how much it would have cost to purchase the same basket of goods in the other year. The ratio between these sums of money is a measure of the average change in prices between one year and the other.

Suppose the cost of the basket was $1.20 in the first year and $1.26 in the second. The ratio is then $126/120 = 1.05$. It is convenient in practice to write this multiplied by 100 (in order to avoid unnecessary writing of decimal points); so we say that the index-number of prices in the second year (with the first as base) is 105. The index-number in the base year must of course be 100.

Every index-number of prices is based upon a particular basket; but of course if we take a different basket we may get a rather different index-number—a rather different measure for the relative change in prices. Special index-numbers for 'deflating' different components of the national product to comparability through time have been developed by Dr.

[2] It is important that the *qualities* of these goods should be as similar as possible in the two years.

Simon Kuznets and by the Department of Commerce. The authors tell us, however, that these index-numbers are somewhat imperfect for their own purposes; and of course no one index can serve all purposes. To illustrate, students who are interested (as many have been in recent years) in the relation between 'disposable income' and the net savings of individuals would be well advised to treat all disposable income as potential consumption, and to deflate disposable income, consumption, and savings by the index-number appropriate to consumption. On the other hand, students who are interested in the performance of an economy over time would be well advised to deflate the excess of national product over consumption (i.e. investment and government) by index-numbers reflecting the prices of new houses, industrial plant, etc., and the costs of government service.[3]

4. WEIGHTS

The method of calculating an index-number which is employed in practice is slightly different from that which we have described, though it comes to identically the same thing. The situation in the base year is first examined, and the proportions of the total cost of the basket which are due to each of the separate articles are first calculated. These proportions are called *weights*. A simple example is set out in the table on page 205. The basket is supposed, for simplicity, to contain only three sorts of goods, in the stated quantities. If the prices in the base year are as stated, the total values of these amounts

[3] An interesting example of the possible need to apply different measurements to the same data for different purposes is afforded by Dr. Simon Kuznets' Occasional Paper No. 6 (1942), dealing with national output over a span from 1879 through 1938. The series in '1929 dollars' shows a marked uptrend of consumption relative to investment. But the series in 'current dollars' shows that the proportion of the product represented by investment has no strong trend from decade to decade. Either observation taken alone would misrepresent the situation; no one pair of series for consumption and investment could do justice to the record.

can be calculated by multiplication, and the total value of the whole basket by adding up the value column. Dividing each of the separate values by their total, and multiplying by 100, we have the weights.

	Quantities	Base year prices	Total value	Weights	
Bread	3 loaves	8 cents per loaf	$0.24	100 × (.24/1.20) =	20
Milk	3 quarts	12 cents per quart	.36	100 × (.36/1.20) =	30
Beef	1½ pounds	40 cents per pound	.60	100 × (.60/1.20) =	50
			$1.20		100

Now pass on to the other year, which is to be compared with the base year. Suppose that in this other year the prices of the three articles were as set out in the second table which now follows. If we recalculated the total value of our basket at the new prices, we should find that it came out to $1.26. The required index-number of price change could be calculated directly by dividing this sum by $1.20. But when there are a large number of different articles in the basket, and particularly when it is desired to calculate a whole series of index-numbers for different years on the same base, it is often more convenient to reach the same result in a different way. We reckon what is the proportionate change in the price of each of the articles between the two years, expressing this in the form of a separate index-number for each article. Then we multiply each of the separate index-numbers by its corresponding weight, add up, and divide by 100.

	Second year prices	Separate index numbers	Separate index numbers × weights	
Bread	7 cents per loaf	(7/8) × 100 = 87.5	87.5 × 20 =	1,750
Milk	13 cents per quart	(13/12) × 100 = 108.36	108.36 × 30 =	3,252
Beef	44 cents per pound	(44/40) × 100 = 110.0	110.0 × 50 =	5,500
			100)10,502	
			105	

Whichever method of calculation we employ, the cost of purchasing the basket has risen by 5 per cent between one year and the other; so the index-number of the second year (on the first as base) is 105.

5. THE COST-OF-LIVING INDEX

The most widely known and used American index-number is the official index of the cost of living, published by the Bureau of Labor Statistics on a monthly basis. The basket of goods on which this index is based is supposed to represent that consumed in a week by a typical wage-earner's or low-salaried clerical worker's family. It is thus an index of very fundamental importance. The prices whose movement it covers fairly directly are the important prices for the great bulk of the population; and between the importance of these same prices for the groups not directly represented (the upper-income groups in cities and the farmers) and the rough parallelism in the movement of other prices, the index is a respectable substitute for a more precise deflator both for consumption as a whole and for the national product, if used for years fairly close together.

For many years the index was based on an investigation of the costs of working-class living in 1913. In recent years it has been revised and placed on a 1935-9 base in the light of more recent studies, including the large-scale investigation of Consumer Purchases in 1935-6. Price quotations are assembled from a number of different cities. Critical studies in connection with wage stabilization disputes in 1943 and 1944 have brought out the defects which result from failure to allow fully for the shifting importance of different types of shops and for migration among centers with different levels of living costs, for the effect of 'sales' at reduced prices, etc. But in general the index has stood examination very well.

The parallel index of living costs for wage-earners in Britain is still based on 1904 food data and 1914 data for other components. A study was made in 1937-8 as basis for a revision, which was delayed by the outbreak of war.[4] Pro-

[4] *Ministry of Labour Gazette,* December 1940 and January-February 1941.

fessor A. L. Bowley [5] has calculated, however, that a revision of weights on the new basis would have changed the 1937-8 level (1914 = 100) only from 157 to 159. This small divergence is certainly a tribute to the British index—or perhaps rather to the foolproof character of this type of index-number.

6. INDEX-NUMBERS OF WHOLESALE PRICES

The cost-of-living index is an index of retail prices—that is, of the prices people actually pay in the shops. For purposes of reducing the national income to real terms, this makes it a more satisfactory index than most of the other index-numbers of prices which receive attention; for they are index-numbers of wholesale prices [6]—of the prices of raw materials, and of goods sold by one firm to another. Nevertheless, while we are on the subject, something may usefully be said about some of these other index-numbers.

Perhaps the most famous of wholesale index-numbers is the Sauerbeck index for Great Britain, published nowadays by the *Statist* newspaper.[7] The principal virtue of the Sauerbeck index is that it goes back a long way, having been compiled in the same way ever since 1846. In its method of construction it is exceedingly crude; the different prices included in it are not weighted at all, but the separate index-numbers for the separate goods are just added up and averaged. There is a basket of goods implied in the Sauerbeck index, as in other index-numbers; but it is an extremely odd basket, arrived at by accident, and without economic significance.

[5] *Review of Economic Studies,* June 1941, p. 134.

[6] It should not be supposed that an index of 'wholesale prices' is simply an index of the prices at which retailers buy the goods whose retail prices enter the cost of living. Some such prices are included; but the general basis of inclusion in a wholesale index is availability of clear-cut quotations on a standardized quality basis, which results in loading the indices unduly with such commodities as grains, fibers, and staple metals—largely but not entirely goods with unusually wide price fluctuations.

[7] Also in the *Journal of the Royal Statistical Society.*

In the United States, the best index-number of wholesale prices (as of the cost of living) is that of the Bureau of Labor Statistics. This index has very wide coverage since 1919, and has been carried back with a smaller list of commodities to

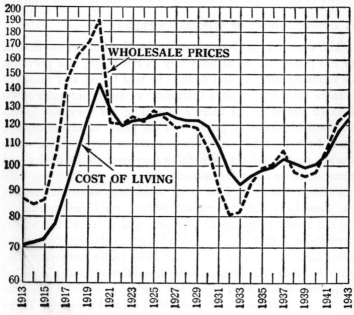

CHART III. WHOLESALE PRICES AND COST OF LIVING IN U.S.A., 1913-43; 1935-9 = 100

1890. By the use of scattered newspaper quotations for a few commodities, an extension as far back as 1793 has been calculated; but such a historical *tour de force* must not be taken as the equivalent of sober calculation for a period short enough to be internally comparable and recent enough to afford ample source material.

The movements of the two official American indices since 1913 are shown graphically in Chart III. It will be noticed that the two indices usually move in the same direction, but the wholesale index is more 'sensitive'—its movements are more violent. It is everywhere the usual experience that wholesale prices are more sensitive than retail; there are a good many reasons for this, one of the simplest being that wholesale prices are more directly affected by such disturbances as harvest fluctuations. The price of apples (say) to the final consumer equals the wholesale price *plus* an extra (often a large extra) to cover the costs of transport, marketing, and final sale; if there was a great overproduction of apples, the wholesale price might be halved, but much the same extra would still be adding for selling costs, and so the retail price might fall by no more than a quarter. Wholesale prices are also affected, more directly than retail, by those instabilities in the production of new capital goods, which we discussed in an earlier chapter.[8] These matters deserve a good deal of attention, but a full examination of them requires other methods than those which we are using in this volume.

[8] See above, ch. VIII.

XVI

NATIONAL INCOME AND ECONOMIC PROGRESS

1. How Far the National Income Can Be Used to Measure Economic Progress

When the national income has been converted into real terms (when those changes which are solely due to changes in the prices at which goods are valued have been so far as possible eliminated) it provides us with the best single measure of the nation's economic well-being, or economic progress, which we are likely to be able to get. Of course no single measure can tell us all we should like to know; the national income only measures the total volume of goods and services at the disposal of the community during the year; it can tell us nothing, for example, about the way in which that total amount is divided up between rich and poor.[1] Even apart from this question of distribution, the national income has other imperfections which we have noted as we went along, and which we should now do well to recall to our memory. In the first place, the services which are included in the national income are only those services which are paid for, and these do not include all the useful work which is performed.[2] Secondly, no attention is paid to the effort of labor; an increase in the national income which came about as the result of longer hours being worked would not be an unqualified gain in economic welfare.[3] Thirdly, there is the awkward

[1] We shall be discussing this matter in the following chapter.
[2] See above, pp. 29-30.
[3] See above, pp. 92-3.

question about some of the public services, whether they are to be regarded as directly useful in themselves, or as means to the production of things which are directly useful.[4] An increase in production which took the form of an increased output of services needed for order and defense might not be a clear economic gain like other increases in production. Finally, there is the makeshift character of our devices for eliminating changes in prices. All these imperfections need to be borne in mind when we seek to use the variations in the real national income as a measure of economic progress. Fortunately, over the period of years which we shall be considering in this chapter, they are none of them likely to be very seriously upsetting.[5]

There is, however, one other imperfection which needs separate consideration, because (though we have not allowed for it yet) it can be corrected for without serious difficulty. This is the matter of population. Obviously, if the working population of a country is rising, we should expect the real national income to rise with it; more hands should produce more goods. If the national income remained steady when the working population was rising, the position would not be a stationary one; it would be seriously deteriorating. For purposes of comparing economic welfare at different times, it is average real income *per head* which is the interesting figure, not total real income. But probably not real income per head of the *total* population. For let us suppose that population began to increase as a result of people having larger families. So long as the extra inhabitants were in the cradle, or even while they were at school, there would be more mouths to feed (and this would be important), but we should not expect to get any increase in the national output, and consequently in the national income, until they arrived at an age

4 See above, p. 175.
5 For some discussions of the parallel problem of comparing the economic well-being of different countries, see Appendix, Note F.

to start working. The fall in the national income per head of total population which might take place in the intervening period would not indicate that the nation was economically going downhill. In order to avoid misapprehensions of this sort, it seems better to divide the national income not by the total population, but by the *occupied* population [6] (those who are either working or seeking work). Occupied population will exclude children, women working in the home, and old people (and these are properly excluded, since we should not expect them to contribute to the national output); it includes the unemployed (who are seeking work, but cannot get it), and it would seem to be quite proper for the unemployed to be included, since a fall in national income due to an increase in the numbers of workers unemployed does mark a real decline in the efficiency of production. Let us therefore take as our test of economic progress the movement of real national income per head of occupied population.[7]

2. REAL AND MONEY INCOME BETWEEN THE WORLD WARS

For the United States, Dr. Simon Kuznets' calculations for the National Bureau of Economic Research give us a series of national income figures for 1919-38, and calculations of the

[6] See above, ch. VI.

[7] This means the number in the labor force, including unemployed, and is on the whole the most satisfactory basis for measuring economic performance; but there are other ways of measuring population which are more appropriate for other purposes. To gauge economic welfare, for instance, it would be preferable to measure population in 'consuming units,' giving different weights to different individuals according to age and other factors affecting their consumption requirements. To gauge changes in productivity, the number actually at work (reduced to 'full-time equivalents' at a constant standard work-week) is more serviceable. The simple number of persons changes nearly enough in proportion to occupied population and to consuming units to make 'per capita' figures fairly adequate substitutes for measuring changes over short periods within a given country; but 'per capita' comparisons are likely to be very misleading as between countries, or as between periods a decade or more apart, or where the number actually at work comes in question.

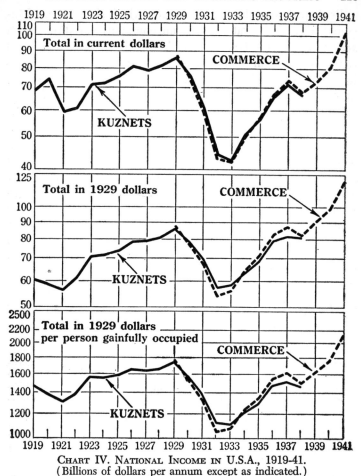

CHART IV. NATIONAL INCOME IN U.S.A., 1919-41.
(Billions of dollars per annum except as indicated.)

U.S. Department of Commerce a series for 1929 and succeeding years. Adjusting both these series to the definition of national income used in this book [8] gives the result shown in Chart IV.

[8] Dr. Kuznets' series (*National Income and Its Composition*, New York, 1941) is increased by the amount of taxes on corporate profits and

Beginning with the highest curves, which show nominal income, it is plain that there is an enormous variation. From 1929 to 1933 there is a drop of almost exactly half; from 1933 to the early wartime levels of 1941, a rise to well over the 1929 level, or 2.4 times that of 1933. Reference to the second curve, however, shows that a good part of this fluctuation reflects the variability of the dollar with which nominal income is measured. In '1929 dollars,' the Kuznets series shows the 1929-33 drop as one-third instead of one-half; and the Commerce series shows the 1933-41 rise as reaching 2.1 times (rather than 2.4 times) the 1933 level.[9] The third pair of curves, which allows for the growth of the occupied population, shows substantially the same year-to-year shifts as the second; but the growth of occupied population (which rose from 41.3 million in 1919 to 55.1 million in 1938, according to the series used by Dr. Kuznets [10] is sufficient to tilt the right-hand end of the curves rather sharply downward. This third pair of curves conveys an impression of rapid and on the whole fairly steady progress during the 1920's, broken by the

decreased by the amount of 'government savings' to give a series on this basis. The Department of Commerce series (*Survey of Current Business*) is increased by the amount of corporate taxes and the estimated rental value of owner-occupied homes, and decreased by the amount of business profits arising from revaluation of inventories. While there are some differences between the resulting series in the period of overlap (1929-38) they are not in general serious enough to affect interpretation fundamentally.

[9] The Kuznets series is 'deflated' by the use of Dr. Kuznets' own index, which is based on careful consideration of the price changes in all the types of goods making up the national product. The Commerce series is much more crudely deflated, being simply divided by the Bureau of Labor Statistics cost of living index. Actually the price increase from 1933 to 1943 was somewhat larger, and the increase of national income measured in 'dollars of constant purchasing power' somewhat smaller than the use of this index implies.

[10] Works Progress Administration, National Research Project, *Labor Supply and Employment,* 1939. Other estimates show very similar trends. Note that the series is for persons 'gainfully occupied,' which includes self-employed, employees, and unemployed. Rough guesses have been made to extend this series to 1939-41.

great depression of the 1930's. The recovery from this depression did not bring the real national income per person gainfully occupied back to the level of 1929 until 1940, nor back into line with the rate of growth appearing in the 1920's until 1941.[11] The experience of 1941 and of the war years shows plainly that the discouraging record of the 1930's did not reflect a cessation of growth in the nation's capacity to produce, but rather the unemployment of a good fraction of labor and other resources. The national product of 1939, which was about as large as that of 1929 with price correction, was produced by several million fewer workers, working considerably shorter hours per week. At the same time, the available labor force had grown, and unemployment in 1939 was in the neighborhood of 10 million.

3. FLUCTUATIONS IN REAL INCOME

To attempt a proper explanation of the dips and rises in the real income curve would involve us in matters which lie outside the scope of this book. The immediate cause of the 1920-21 drop, the drop from 1929 to 1933, the drop from 1937 to 1938, and the arrested growth from 1923 to 1924 and from 1926 to 1927 was a slump in employment; the immediate cause of the rise from 1921 to 1923 and 1924 to 1925, and of the recovery from 1933 onward was an improvement in employment. But the causes of unemployment and of improvements in employment are hard to explain.

Without trying to go too deep, it is plain that the great depression after 1929 reflected the difficulties in maintaining an even flow of capital goods to which we referred in an earlier

[11] It is important to remember that different countries show very different developments. In Britain, for example, there was a discouraging period of arrested growth in the 1920's; the dip in real income in the early 1930's was very mild (thanks largely to the fact that food and other British imports fell much more sharply in price than did British exports); and there was a buoyant rise during the 1930's.

chapter,[12] compounded and intensified by a serious collapse in our monetary arrangements and by a profound and widespread loss of 'confidence.' There is good reason to suspect that the adjustments by which the flow of capital goods was maintained during the 1920's were inherently unstable; and neither the 1930's nor the war can possibly have placed the nation in a position where more stable adjustments will come about smoothly or automatically. It remains for postwar experience to show how well the United States can organize itself for full and stable employment.

4. GROWTH IN PRODUCTIVITY

So much for the dips. But the economic development of the United States during this period contained more than dips and rises: there was also the underlying upward trend in productive power, however imperfectly it was realized in the 1930's. What can we say about the underlying causes of this trend?

To begin with, it must be understood that an upward trend of real income per gainfully occupied person has been of long standing in the United States. The tradition of continuous progress from the first settlements is something of an exaggeration. Materials for a reasonably reliable measurement of national income and output begin only about 1880; but it is plain that there were earlier periods of rapid economic progress and other periods of 'hard times' in which output only kept pace with the growth of population, or even lost ground. For the period 1879-1938, Dr. Kuznets has worked out national-product estimates not for each year but for each decade. The result is clear evidence of a vigorous growth during 1879-1928, with a strong suggestion that the rate of growth in real income per person gainfully occupied reached a peak about 1913. Growth during the 1920's, however—or the growth registered from 1929 to 1942—is at rates fully com-

[12] Ch. VIII.

parable with those of 1879-1913, suggesting no slackening in the growth of productive capacity.

Remembering our general plan of the productive process, it is plain at first sight that this gradual upward movement in real income per head must be due to some combination of three causes: (1) improvements in the average skill of labor, (2) increases in the capital equipment worked, with (3) improvements in technique—the utilization of more efficient methods of combining labor with capital. Is it possible to say anything about the relative importance of these causes in this particular case?

As far as present knowledge goes, it is not possible to say very much, though further investigation may well throw more light on the matter. Something can plausibly be ascribed to improvements in the average skill of labor. Education (both general and technical) has been very greatly improved during the present century. A much larger proportion of all workers are carrying their education past the elementary level. Since a great proportion of the labor force always consists of workers whose training was at the older and lower standards, this is just the sort of slow-acting cause one would expect to be connected with an upward trend in productive power. Besides the effects of formal education, allowance must be made for the diffusion of such unobtrusive skills as the ability to drive an automobile in traffic (which is an excellent training in co-ordinating the use of mechanical controls, adapting to visible and audible signals, and watching for signs of a machine getting out of adjustment), reading road maps, and learning to follow instructions in order to learn an operation quickly. While it is true that many of the traditional skills are losing value, it is equally true that new skills are being developed; and there are few workers who are 'unskilled' in the sense that applied in the nineteenth century to immigrants who had no experience with industrial society, and for this reason and because of language barriers could not deal with complicated instructions.

Improvements due to increases in capital equipment and improvements due to advances in technique are hard to disentangle. We do possess some estimates of the rate of capital accumulation during the period; [13] but there is a good deal of uncertainty about them, and they are not easy to interpret. Taken at their face value, the figures would seem to suggest that investment in new capital has been quite sufficient over the period for a considerable part of the increase in real income to be properly attributable to this cause.[14] The statistical evidence which leads to this conclusion is not very strong; but this is one of the cases in which we may reasonably have more confidence in the conclusion than in the statistics. For in a period of advancing technique, the effectiveness of new additions to capital is always greater than it appears to be, judging simply by the value of the additions. The increase of capital equipment does not merely consist of new capital goods being added to the old, new goods which are of the same sorts as the old; the additional capital goods are to a large extent goods of different sorts, more up-to-date sorts, which generally means more efficient sorts. The same thing applies indeed to the replacements of capital which take place during the period. Capital goods wear out and are replaced; but an old machine is not necessarily replaced by the same sort of machine as before. If there has been an improvement in technical methods in the interval since the old machine was acquired, the new machine is likely to be different from the old, more efficient than the old. The new machine may sometimes cost no more than the old machine which it replaces, so that the firm which uses it does not reckon that

[13] See Simon Kuznets, *Occasional Paper No. 6* (National Bureau of Economic Research, 1942).

[14] Dr. Kuznets' figures indicate between 2½ and 3 times as much available in the way of durable-use producers' goods (including housing) per 'producing unit' of labor, in 1929-38 as in 1879-88.

it has made any addition to its capital; but if it is more efficient than the old machine which it replaces, there is an increase in productivity, due (perhaps we may say) to an improvement in the *quality* of the capital equipment employed.

Improvements in technique do very commonly take the form of improvements in the quality of capital. The making of an invention—the *discovery* of a more efficient method of production—does not itself increase productivity; productivity is only increased when the new method is applied, and usually it cannot be applied until the new equipment with which to apply it has been constructed. Thus it frequently happens that increases in productivity which are ultimately due to a particular invention are not completed until several decades after the date when the invention was originally made. Probably the most potent of the inventions which increased productivity between the two great wars were the internal-combustion engine and the electric dynamo; but neither of these was a new invention; each was inherited from the nineteenth century and had completed all the essential stages of its technical development before 1910; the great economic effects of these inventions belong to the later period, because the inventions had to be embodied in capital goods before they could be utilized, and the new capital goods took time to construct. It is well to remind ourselves of the variety of capital goods which are needed for the full utilization of a major invention like the internal-combustion engine. Even in the field of terrestrial locomotion alone, it was not merely a question of making the motor-trucks and motor-buses, the motor-cars and motor-bicycles; the plant for making these vehicles had first to be constructed, while garages to repair them were also necessary, paved roads on which they could run, tankers and pipe-lines to bring them their fuel, and gasoline pumps from which to distribute it. And none of these things could function unless there were also available the oil-wells from which the essential fuel originally springs, and the tropical plantations to provide rubber for the tires. When one remembers that only a limited proportion of the community's resources is available each year for new investment, and that there are other forms of new investment to be provided for as well (in our period the most important of these competing forms of new investment was housing), it is not surprising that a great invention should take some time to realize itself fully. But while it is realizing itself, it adds very greatly to the productivity of the additions to capital which are being made.

XVII

THE INEQUALITY OF INCOMES

1. INEQUALITY AMONG AND WITHIN SOCIAL GROUPS

In our studies of the national income, we have divided it up in various ways: into the part which is consumed and the part which is saved, into the part which is taken by the State and the part which is left in private hands, into the part which is paid for personal services and the part which is paid for the services of property. But so far we have said scarcely anything about what most people would regard as the most interesting sort of division—the division into large and small incomes. This division carries important clues not only to the problem of poverty, but also to the problem of inequality in political power.

The extremes of the income distribution are very far apart. In every year a few incomes are reported which exceed $1,000,000; and on account of business losses there are always some incomes far below zero. But negative incomes are very few relative to large incomes; and in consequence the presence of large incomes pulls the average income up, and about two-thirds of all families have incomes below the average, while 5 per cent or somewhat more have incomes exceeding double the average.

The latest and for most purposes the most satisfactory study of income size distribution in the United States is the official 'Survey of Spending and Saving in Wartime,' based on a sample of incomes for 1941. The results are summed up in Table VII. It will be seen that at the very bottom of the scale the distribution thickens as we go up the scale; incomes below

TABLE VII

Percentages of Families, of Aggregate Money Income, and of Aggregate Consumer Expenditure, by Family Income, 1941

Money income per family	Percentage allocation of		
	Families	Money income	Consumer expenditure
Below $ 500	16	2	4
$ 500 to 1,000	18	7	8
1,000 to 1,500	16	10	11
1,500 to 2,000	14	13	14
2,000 to 3,000	21	26	27
3,000 to 5,000	11	20	20
over $5,000	4	22	16
All families	100	100	100

$500 were less common than incomes between $500 and $1,000. But beginning at a very modest level indeed, the numbers begin to taper off. In 1941, incomes between $500 and $1,000 were more common than incomes between $1,000 and $1,500, which in turn were more common than incomes between $1,500 and $2,000; incomes between $1,000 and $2,000 were more common than between $2,000 and $3,000—and so it goes clear up the income scale. This distribution is on a family basis (single persons not living in families being treated as 'one-person families'). But if it were stated in terms of individual income recipients, while the number of incomes shown would be greater in total and somewhat less (on account of family incomes being splintered up among two or more recipients) in the high brackets, the general picture of inequality would give much the same impression.

The upper end of the income distribution is made up largely of people owning a great deal of property (and generally having also large earnings from salary or unincorporated business), and the lower end is made up largely of low-income farmers, families on relief, and elderly people in retirement. But inequality is at least as important within social groups as between groups; and separate distributions of income by size drawn up for such groups overlap. This may be seen from Table VIII, which gives figures drawn from the 'Consumer Purchases Study' of 1935-6. While the most common income for wage-earner families at that time appears as around $1,000 per year and for salaried business and professional families around $2,000, for example, there was a sprinkling of professional families below $1,000 and more than a sprinkling of wage-earner families above $2,000.

2. CAUSES OF INEQUALITY: DIFFERENCES IN EARNINGS, DIFFERENCES IN PROPERTY OWNERSHIP; ACQUISITION OF PROPERTY

What are the reasons for the inequality of incomes? This is a very wide question; we have to draw upon many branches of economics before we can answer it properly, and only a beginning can be made here.

As soon as we begin to think about the question systematically, it becomes clear that it can be divided, more or less completely, into a number of sub-questions. Since incomes are derived either from the earnings of labor or from the ownership of capital, we have to ask: (1) why some people have larger personal earnings than others; (2) why some people own more capital than others; (3) why the proportions going to labor and capital respectively are as they are.

Some of the reasons for differences in the wages earned by different people for the work they do have already been discussed to some extent in earlier chapters.[1] We have seen that the economic functions of differences in wages are to facili-

[1] Chs. VI and VII above.

TABLE VIII

Number of Families by Income Level and by Occupation Yielding Bulk of Income, 1935-6
(thousands)

Income per family	Families receiving some relief during year	Families receiving no relief, by major income source						Total
		Wages	Clerical salary	Self-employment Farm	Other	Salary-business and professional	Property and other	
Below $ 500	1,524	993	80	1,091	182	28	280	4,178
$ 500 to 1,000	1,920	2,668	501	2,136	480	123	249	8,076
1,000 to 1,500	780	2,742	862	1,395	559	279	131	6,748
1,500 to 2,000	155	1,626	841	731	427	403	57	4,240
2,000 to 3,000	108	1,121	920	518	463	596	50	3,779
3,000 to 5,000	0	290	356	209	291	407	35	1,595
Over $5,000	0	19	66	87	312	266	44	794
All levels	4,487	9,459	3,626	6,167	2,714	2,102	846	29,400

tate the distribution of labor among occupations, and to provide an incentive to effort. If an adequate supply of particular sorts of work is difficult to get, and there are particular people who are specially suitable to perform these kinds of work, there is a case for giving them a wage sufficient to induce them to specialize themselves, and to exert themselves, in these occupations. Some differences in wages can be defended on these grounds; but it must not be supposed that all the differences which exist at any particular time can be defended in this way. For example, it often happens that a high level of wages is established in a particular occupation, in the first place for good reasons; but after a time the labor needed ceases to be specially scarce, and yet the high wages may persist. Once people have acquired a privileged position, they are reluctant to abandon it, and will use all sorts of economic and political pressure to maintain it. The branch of economics which deals with differences in earnings from labor is therefore concerned both with discovering what differences can be justified on grounds of efficiency, and with criticizing the differences that actually exist by comparing them with more ideal arrangements.

Inequality in earnings results not only from differences in wage-rates but from differences in ability to find work. Except in wartime, a good part of the working force is affected by unemployment during part of the year, and unemployment affects different people very unevenly. On the other hand, some family incomes are made up by the combined earnings of several family members. Most of the wage-earning and clerical families toward the upper end of the income scale in 1935-6 (see Table VIII) and in 1941 were there because they were so fortunate as to have several employable members.

The proportion in which the national income is divided between capital and labor raises issues similar to those involved in the inequality of wage rates. This is one of the most important of economic problems, but it is also one of the most difficult, and it is not even yet completely settled. It would be impossible to say anything useful about it with the methods we are using in this book.

Inequality in capital ownership is perhaps the most striking of the three elements which are responsible for the inequality of incomes. If the ownership of capital were equally distributed, the fact that a considerable proportion of the national income is taken in profits would matter far less; and since nearly all the largest incomes are due to the ownership of large amount of capital, the disparity between the largest and the smallest incomes would be far less wide. Inequality in the ownership of capital is indeed one of the things which make for inequality in the earnings of labor; people who possess capital (or whose parents possess capital) find it easier to enter some of the more remunerative occupations, and in other ways have wider fields for the exercise of such talents as they possess. If capital were more equally distributed, a great deal of the problem of inequality would disappear.

Capital is acquired in two main ways—by personal saving and by inheritance. The small savings which the ordinary man puts aside for his old age, or as a nest-egg against emergencies, do in the end make him into a capitalist, though a very modest one. The successful man, on the other hand, who earns a large income from his labor, but spends only a small part of that income, may become a capitalist on a considerable scale long before the end of his working life; this is particularly likely to be the case if his talents are of a kind which enable him to invest his capital profitably, and so get a large return on it from the start. To acquire a really large amount of capital entirely from one's own savings is, however, very exceptional; the wholly 'self-made' captain of industry is rarer in the twentieth century than he was in the nineteenth. Generally it takes two or three generations to build up the largest estates; it is very hard to build up a great fortune if you start from scratch, but if you have some (even a moderate) start in the race it is much easier. The part played by inheritance of property in causing inequality of capital ownership is therefore a very important one.

The acquisition of capital by inheritance is usually regarded nowadays [2] as less justifiable than acquisition by personal saving; the State has therefore considered that the passage of property at death is a suitable occasion for special taxation. The American federal government began to tax estates in 1916; but until 1932 rates remained low enough so that the tax probably affected the inequality of capital ownership only very slightly. Rates were increased in 1932, 1934, 1935, and 1941. The 1941 rates are substantial for really enormous estates. For example, an estate of $50,000,000 would be reduced to $1,000,000 by five successive transfers at death—on condition that a single heir received the whole remaining property on each occasion, and that nothing was added by savings on the part of the heirs. Estates which are large but not enormous are much less strongly affected. For example, it would take 15 successive transfers at death (which normally would represent at least four centuries) to reduce a $5,000,000 estate to $100,000. Furthermore, it must not be supposed that the whole estate is taxable at these rates whenever the owner dies. Transfers by gift go at lower rates. When a large fortune is more or less evenly spread among family members (as many now are), only a fraction of the total property of the family is affected by any one death. By use of trust funds, moreover, transfers subject to tax can be made to take place only once in two or three generations. Estate taxes as hitherto applied are thus calculated to spread property somewhat more evenly within the property-owning class, but are not able to

[2] In earlier times it would not have been regarded in that light.

affect very sharply the inequality between the group owning large fortunes and the rest of the population.[3]

3. EFFECTS OF TAXES AND GOVERNMENT EXPENDITURES ON INEQUALITY

Inequality of incomes can of course be more directly affected by taxes falling on current incomes and by social expenditure. Indirect taxes, since they fall largely on consumption (which is larger in relation to income at low than at high brackets), tend to increase inequality; and so do payments of interest on the national debt, which go primarily to the higher brackets. On the other hand, taxes on corporate profits affect chiefly the higher incomes, since the ownership of corporate shares is associated with high incomes; and besides estate taxes, taxes on personal incomes fall in large part on the higher incomes. On the expenditure side, public provision of free education, free health services, free recreation, and assistance in housing benefit the lower income groups more than the upper (not merely in proportion to income, but in proportion to numbers); such transfer payments as relief and old-age assistance go entirely to the lowest income groups. Social Security provisions for unemployment and old age will in the end work out largely as transfers among the working population; but contributions will be larger than benefits for the more prosperous and smaller for the less prosperous. On the whole the influence of government finance is towards equalization of incomes available after subtraction of taxes and contributions and addition of transfer payments.

This influence must not be exaggerated. At prewar tax levels, in 1939, taxes on estates, personal incomes, and corporate profits were only about 4.2 per cent of income pay-

[3] In England, a comparison by H. Campion (*Public and Private Property*, pp. 108-10) is inconclusive as to whether the concentration of wealth was greater in 1913 than 20 to 25 years later, although fairly substantial taxes were levied on inheritances between the two dates.

ments, and Social Security contributions (including those of employers) about 2.6 per cent; on the other hand, all transfer payments amounted to 4.7 per cent (of which 1.3 per cent represented Social Security, and 1.4 per cent represented interest on the national debt). These magnitudes are enough to account for a large reduction in the small relative share of the few thousand most prosperous families at the top of the scale, and a large increase in the small relative share of the few million least prosperous families at the bottom; but for income levels from $1,000 to $25,000 (say) the effect on relative shares was mild. With the likelihood of higher tax rates and a more highly developed Social Security system after the war, the impact of government finance will be more strongly felt.[4]

4. EXTENT OF 'SURPLUS CONSUMPTION' BY THE WEALTHY

As may be seen from Table VII, consumer expenditure is considerably more equally distributed than is income. For example, the poorest 34 per cent of families had only 9 per cent of the aggregate money income; but they accounted for 12 per cent of aggregate money expenditure on consumption, or for 15 per cent of expenditure if the non-cash items of rent-free housing and home-raised food are included. At the other end of the scale, the richest 4 per cent of families had 22 per cent of aggregate money income, but only 16 per cent of

[4] Interwar experience in Britain may give some indication of postwar prospects here. According to figures presented in the English edition of this book, direct taxes in 1938 were 11.2 per cent of the nominal incomes of individuals (as against 4.2 per cent in the United States in 1939) and transfers excluding both the national debt service and social insurance amounted to 5.5 per cent (as against about 2.0 per cent in the United States in 1939). Allowing for indirect as well as direct taxes, incomes which before tax adjustments were under £250 are estimated for 1937 to have been 57.4 per cent of the British national total before allowance for taxes and social expenditures, 65.8 per cent after that allowance. After tax allowance only, the corresponding percentage is 60.1 per cent.

money expenditures and only 14 per cent of expenditure with the non-cash items included.

These differences are due to a number of factors. To begin with, as we have seen, taxes absorb a noticeable proportion of income at the highest levels. In the second place, philanthropic gifts are also larger relative to income at high income levels. In the third place, the proportion of income saved varies sharply with income. This is due partly to the obvious fact that a high level of personal prosperity makes it easier to save and even imposes special social pressures to do so; partly to the fact that a good proportion of the families at the extremes of the income scale are there only temporarily. Field investigations regularly find that families with very low incomes have 'negative savings'—that is, spend more than they receive—and such a situation reflects either spending from the accumulations of earlier prosperity or using credit based on expectations of prosperity in future. Similarly, a good proportion of those reporting high incomes in a particular year are in receipt of some unusual gain which naturally is largely saved. The greater equality in expenditure which appears where non-cash items are included reflects the fact that many low-income consumers live in rural and small-town conditions, where they can readily own their own homes and keep gardens, while many high-income consumers do not bother to raise food, etc., even if they can. If it were possible to include a fair value for the household services of women, the degree of apparent inequality would be further reduced.

The limited extent to which the 'poor' could conceivably gain from redistributing the incomes of the 'rich' may also be seen from these figures. A combined income of $5,000 per year is not commonly considered a huge family income. Yet of the 22 per cent of money income shown in Table vii as belonging to those with over $5,000, 10 per cent represents the first $5,000 per family, and only 12 per cent the excess over $5,000; of this excess, taxes captured a considerable share. If we draw the line at $3,000, the total income of those with over $3,000 was 42 per cent; of this 23 per cent represents the first $3,000 per family and 19 per cent the excess over $3,000. If we measure by consumption instead of income, the margins may be seen to be still narrower. For all families with *consumption* over $5,000 per year, the excess over $5,000 probably was closer to 5 per cent of aggregate consumption.

The notion that 'redistributing' income taken (say) from the richest 5 per cent of the people could substantially benefit all of the other 95 per cent is unconvincing in the light of these facts—particularly since socialist societies as well as capitalist societies find it necessary for incentive purposes to let some energetic and efficient members earn several times the average, net of all taxes. Enough can be 'redistributed' to mitigate the extremes of poverty and to set up safeguards against a cumulative concentration of power in the hands of an oligarchy. But substantial economic gains for the majority of the population must be sought in increased productivity and reduced unemployment—in expanding the total of real incomes, not in reapportioning an existing total. 'Redistribution' can aid in some ways towards this goal;[5] but its effects on economic incentives have drawbacks. The decision how far to push measures of this kind is one of the most important, and also one of the most delicate, with which democratic societies are faced.

It is utopian to think in terms of eliminating inequality altogether. Inequality of incomes is one of the major forms taken in our society by a more fundamental inequality—inequality of power. This more fundamental inequality persists in all

---

[5] In particular, it may help to mitigate the effect of poverty in making it hard for many people to get the food, housing, medical care, education, etc., which are necessary to unfold their productive powers. Furthermore, in conditions where uses are not being found for all the savings people are inclined to make, 'redistribution' may make it easier to keep a stoppage of the flow of money payments from leading to unemployment.

societies; it is indeed difficult to see how society could be organized without it. It has taken many forms in the course of history—the control of the master over his slaves, of the feudal baron over his serfs, of the landlord over his tenants, of the employer over his workmen, of the organizer over the members of a party or labor organization, of the state official over private citizens. As inequalities go, inequality of income is a relatively harmless kind; the mere fact that it is so easily capable of being catalogued and measured means that there are ways of keeping it in check. It is important that it should be kept in check. But it is still more important for the future of human freedom that we should not open the door to other devils in its place.

FURTHER HORIZONS

There have been several occasions in this book (most frequently in the later chapters) when we have encountered questions—questions of great interest and importance—which we have been obliged to leave unanswered, or to answer in what was obviously a makeshift manner. There was a reason for this—not merely the reason that the book was growing long enough for its purpose, but a more fundamental reason. Although the reader who has mastered what has been set before him will have learned a good deal of economics, the economics he has learned will be all on one side of the subject. A question such as that which arose in our discussion of the causes of inequality (why the national income is divided between wages and profits in the proportions that it is) cannot be answered along the lines we have been following. The same applies to the reasons for the differences in the earnings of different kinds of labor, and to the reasons for changes in the terms of trade. We had to be very sketchy in our discussion of these matters, although they embody economic problems of the first importance. There are branches of economics which do deal with them in detail, but they are different branches of economics from that which we have been studying.

The relation between our branch (which might be called Social Accounting) and the rest of economics can be made clear by an analogy from another science. The study of the human body is divided into two main parts—anatomy and physiology. Anatomy deals with the structure of the body, the various organs and their relations, the plan of the organism as it is discovered by dissection after death. Physiology is concerned with the working of the organism—the living body as a going concern. What we have been studying in this book is economic anatomy, the structure of the body economic, as it can be discovered by statisticians working on figures collected *after the event*. Only very casually have we learned anything about economic physiology—the way the economic system works. Yet economic science cannot get on without its physiological branch; [1] there are indeed many books on elementary economics which deal with little else. It is only as a result of the great advances made in social accounting during the last twenty years that it has been possible to write a book like this which concentrates on the 'anatomical' side; the 'physiological' side was developed earlier, and most elementary books follow that earlier tradition.

I hope the reader will have found that our 'anatomical' method has told him the answers to a good many of the questions he wanted to ask about the economic system when he began his studies; I do not think that so many important questions could have been answered so speedily in any other way. Yet in spite of that it must be insisted that the field we have been covering is only one side of economics; to treat it as more than that would lead to serious error. A striking example of this can be taken from the last chapter. Dissecting the economic system after the event, we can show (as we did) that a certain proportion of the national income was available in a certain year for surplus consumption by the wealthy; it is

[1] Since economic physiology cannot be based upon statistics collected after the event, and since it cannot perform experiments, it is inevitably rather more speculative than a science ideally should be; more of it is *theory*, and less of it is *applied economics*, than one could wish. But this seems to be in the nature of the case, and cannot altogether be helped. Although statistical methods for use on this side of economics have been, and are being devised, the results obtained by their use are rather limited.

easy to jump from that to the conclusion that this surplus could have been taken from the wealthy and distributed among the poorer classes, raising the incomes of the poor by so much per cent. It may well be useful to think the thing out in this way, in order to get an idea of the magnitude of the problem of inequality; but it would be quite wrong to suppose that the transfer could be made in a way which would enable its results to be calculated by simple arithmetic. Some particular device (such as a new tax) would have to be used for making the transference; and no such device can be conceived of, which would not have far-reaching effects on the structure of the whole economic system. The commodities which would be produced in the new circumstances would be different from the commodities which were produced in the old; the incomes earned in producing the new set of commodities would be different from the incomes which were earned in producing the old set. We cannot even be certain, until we have made a special investigation of the matter, whether any particular measure, introduced in order to mitigate the inequality of incomes, will in fact have the effect which is intended.

Many of the most important questions people want to ask about the economic system are questions of the type—*if such and such a thing were done, what would be the probable consequences?* Now hardly any of these questions can be properly answered from a knowledge of social accounting alone. Just as it is impossible to forecast the effect of performing an operation merely from a knowledge of the anatomy of the human body, so it is impossible to forecast the probable effects of an economic reform without having a knowledge of how the economic system works. Therefore, once the student has mastered the groundwork of social accounting, he must go on to the 'physiological' side of economics, whose center is the theory of value. The mechanism by which the economic system works is the system of prices; the fundamental principles of price are what the theory of value studies.

Although the theory of value incorporates so important a body of knowledge, it is perhaps at first sight a less attractive study than social accounting is. The theory of value does reach important conclusions on great questions, but it has to spend a good deal of time on small and apparently trivial questions in order to get there. This is of course a common experience in science; the elementary stages of most sciences are trivial enough. One reason why I have written this book is because I think that a preliminary grasp of social accounting may make the elementary stages of the theory of value easier to bear.

I hope that the reader of this book will come to the end of it with a number of general questions in his mind—questions which were probably not there when he started, questions which have not been answered here, but which he would now like to have answered. Some of these questions may be of the type we have just been discussing—questions of the probable consequences of economic changes. Some may be of other kinds. There are questions concerned with the organization of the economic system; we have seen that more goods and services were produced in some years than others, but could not still more have been produced in any year if things had been organized differently? Then there are questions about definitions: is it really necessary to classify things in the particular compartments we have chosen? Could not the classifications be improved? (A very fundamental question of this last sort is the question whether the money measure of the national income can be justified; if a loaf of bread costs 10¢, and a box of cough drops 5¢, we have taken it that the cough drops represent the same 'output' as half a loaf of bread.) Along some or all of these lines, the intelligent reader will want to criticize; but he has not been given much help towards criticizing. He will find that help if he pursues his studies in the theory of value.

Note A. *On the Definition of Production*

I have kept fairly strictly in this book to the definition of *productive work* as *work done to satisfy the wants of other people through exchange*. This definition corresponds to the definition of income used in this book, and it has the great advantage of being unambiguous. But it is not by any means wholly satisfactory. There are at least three kinds of socially useful work which are excluded from productive work on this definition: (1) domestic work, done within the family, by housewives and others; (2) direct production for use of the family, mainly of foodstuffs, on gardens, allotments, and small-holdings; (3) 'voluntary' work, done for its own sake or from a sense of duty to the community or social group to which one belongs. These kinds of work are only distinguished from the kinds which we do count as productive on the one ground that they are not paid: there is no payment in the ordinary sense, that is, though of course there are other compensations. Exactly similar work can often be found which is paid for; domestic work may be done by a paid housekeeper, the allotment-holder may sell his produce, the club may employ a paid secretary. It would therefore be possible for *production* (in our sense) to go up, merely because some work, which had previously been unpaid, was transferred to the paid class; yet the wants of the community as a whole need not be any better satisfied as a result.

Transferences of this sort do not often occur nowadays on a large scale; but when they do, we must allow for them in some way, if we are not to be led into serious error. It is a serious error, for example, in the economics of war, if we neglect the fact that by drawing women into munition making and other war services the supply of labor for necessary domestic work is diminished. Again, when rapid improvements in transport take place in a hitherto undeveloped country, farmers will change over from producing mainly for their own wants to producing mainly for sale. On our definition of *production* this would cause agricultural production to shoot up from almost nothing to a considerable height; but though the farmers would almost certainly be better off for the change, they would not be as much better off as such figures would indicate. In cases such as this last, there is a great deal to be said for using a wider definition of production, including all agricultural production, whether produced for sale or not; this is in fact what is usually done when estimating the national income of such a country as India. The object of any such calculation is to get the most useful figure possible; in a case where the habit of selling agricultural products is spreading, a figure which includes all such products will be more useful than one which includes only those products which are produced for sale.

It is tempting to seek for a way round the difficulty by widening our definition, including some of the things we have left out; but the trouble then is to know where we should stop. The most promising suggestion for widening is that made (but ultimately rejected for this purpose) by Professor Pigou: [1] that we should include all those kinds of work which can be brought into relation with the 'measuring-rod of money'—not merely those which *are* paid, but those which *might* be paid. Unfortunately it is impossible to interpret this wider definition in a way which would command general agreement. A man might employ a secretary to write his letters; if he writes his own letters, are we to say that the time he spends in doing so is spent in productive work? A man may employ a gardener; if he works in his own garden, how

[1] *Economics of Welfare*, Part i, chs. 1 and 3.

are we to separate out the work which he does to satisfy his own wants for vegetables and flowers, from the work which is an end in itself, which no one could do for him since no one else could give him the pleasure he gets from watching the growth of a shrub, raised from his own cutting and planted by his own hands? The wider definition gets us into inextricable knots; and no other wide definition has been suggested which would not do so. We are therefore driven to adopt the limited definition here used, though we must be prepared to modify it by including some particular things not produced for sale, in cases where it would be seriously misleading not to do so.

It is also interesting to observe that an issue exactly parallel to that which we have discussed in this note arises in another connection.[2] If we decide to reckon as productive only those services of labor which are paid for, we ought to do the same with the services of capital. The durable-use consumers' goods, which are in existence at the beginning of a year, render valuable services to their users during the year; but if user and owner are one and the same person, no payment is made for these services. People derive advantages from the durable-use consumers' goods in their possession, just as they derive advantages from the work which they do to satisfy their own wants; but as we are excluding the one because no payment passes, so it would appear that we must exclude the other. On the same principle, we must include the services of those durable-use consumers' goods for which a rent is paid, since these are analogous to the work which is paid for.

This is the principle; but in this case we meet a difficulty just like that of agricultural production for the farmer's own use. Houses are the most important class of durable-use consumers' goods; but some houses are rented, some are owner-occupied. If we reckoned the services of the rented houses as a part of production, but not the services of the owner-

2 See above, pp. 44-5.

occupied houses (which would be the logical thing to do), we should get into a difficulty just like that which arose over agriculture. An increased tendency for people to own their own houses would appear as a fall in the social income, but it would be absurd to regard it in that light. A change of this sort is decidedly likely. The growth of cities has in the past increased the proportion of people living in rented houses and apartments; decentralization in the future may well reverse this trend.

The inclusion of these rents diverges from the practice of the United States Department of Commerce, but agrees with that of Simon Kuznets. The official reluctance to include house rents appears to rest on no definite ground of principle. It is interesting to note that the 1940 Census classified owner-occupied houses by their estimated rental value, based on the monthly rental paid for similar dwelling units in the neighborhood.

Note B. *On the Idea of an Optimum Population*

When discussing the economics of population in Chapter v, I have carefully avoided making any use of the idea of an Optimum Population, although that idea is widely used in modern discussions of the subject.[3] It is easy to see how the idea arises. If the population of a particular area may be too small for full efficiency of production, and if it may also be too large, it seems there must be some level in between at which it would be *just right*. Could not the same thing be put in more technical language by defining the optimum population as that level of population which would make output per head a maximum? A country would then be called under-populated if its population was less than the optimum, over-populated if its population was more than the optimum.

We have seen that it is possible to give definite and important meanings to the terms under-population and over-

[3] See, for example, Cannan, *Wealth;* Carr-Saunders, *Population.*

population; but this does not suffice to show that an optimum population between the two can be precisely defined. No one has ever been able to say what the optimum population of any particular area is in fact; for this inability there are several very good reasons.

In the first place, what do we mean by saying that *net output per head* is a maximum? The output of society consists not of one good, but of an immense variety of goods and services. In consequence, in order to say that net output per head is greater in one set of circumstances than in another, we have to find a means of reducing the variety of goods to a common measure. Methods of doing this are discussed in Chapter xv; but the methods discussed in that chapter are none of them perfect ways of making the reduction; they are all of them makeshifts. It is not by any means certain that a perfectly suitable method of making the reduction can possibly be found. It is thus extremely probable that a *range* of possible sizes of population would exist, each of which would have a good claim to be regarded as *the* optimum population, if a suitable method of reduction were taken. If population increases, some kinds of goods become harder to get, some become easier; we have got to decide whether the shift from the one sort to the other is advantageous or not, and on that opinions may differ. Sometimes it may be very clear that the advantage exceeds the disadvantage, or vice versa; then we need have no hesitation in saying that the country is underpopulated or overpopulated as the case may be. But between these extremes there is likely to be a range (conceivably quite a wide range) where the advantageousness of a change is largely a matter of opinion. Within this range it would be venturesome to claim that any particular size of population is optimum; it is far more important to notice that it is only when the actual size of population falls outside this range that the size of the population becomes an urgent economic issue.

This is one of the difficulties which has to be borne in mind;

but there are others of greater importance. It is impossible to define the optimum population of an area unless something is taken for granted about the other conditions of economic welfare apart from population. These other conditions include the state of industrial technique, the amount and the character of capital equipment, and the opportunities for external trade. Changes in these other conditions may change the optimum size of population very markedly. England would be grossly overpopulated today if her capital equipment were no greater than it was a century ago; she would be grossly overpopulated today if her opportunities for foreign trade were no greater than they were a century ago. Improvements in industrial technique will usually tend to increase the optimum population of an area.

This being so, an optimum population, defined with reference to the conditions of technique, capital, and foreign trade *as they are at present* is a notion of extremely little practical interest. For in the time which it would inevitably take (by any other route but that of catastrophe) to adjust the actual population to the optimum, we may be sure that the optimum itself would have shifted, and would probably have shifted to an important extent. Further, it is very probable that the optimum size of a population will depend on the age-distribution of that population; but in the process of adjusting the size of population, age-distribution must change. An area could not be said to have reached a fully optimum state of population until its age-distribution was such as to keep the population optimum; but such a condition could hardly be reached from any actual population within a foreseeable future.

These difficulties are not of importance when a country is decidedly under-populated (or over-populated); for we should then be safe in maintaining that an increase (or diminution) of population would still be advantageous, even if the other conditions of production changed in any way that seemed at all probable. But a statement of this sort is not made any clearer by using the phrase 'optimum population.'

Note C. *On the Depreciation of Capital*

The using-up of capital equipment as the result of productive activity takes two forms: (1) the gradual wearing-out of fixed capital—this is what the business man calls depreciation; (2) the using-up of single-use producers' goods—working capital and stocks. Each of these kinds of depreciation raises awkward problems of measurement, perhaps the most awkward of all the problems connected with the national income. Here we can do no more than indicate the general nature of the difficulties.

We have already seen (p. 135 above) that the valuation of a durable-use good, at a time when there is no question of selling it, is always a very delicate matter; different values may be put upon it by different people, and by the same person for different purposes. Naturally the same trouble persists when it is a question of estimating the reduction in the value of a particular piece of equipment, which has resulted from the year's operations: different people might estimate the reduction in different ways. In practice there are two estimates for the depreciation of a firm's fixed capital which need to be carefully distinguished.

In the first place, there is the estimate made by the firm for its own purposes—for example, the purpose of deciding the amount which is available for distribution in dividends. In a well-managed firm, care will usually be taken when framing this estimate to be well on the safe side; when there is any doubt on the matter (as there usually will be) a high figure for depreciation will be chosen rather than a low one. (The systematic choice of high figures for depreciation is the easiest way of setting aside 'hidden reserves.')

The other practically important estimate is that made for

purposes of taxation. Since there is this arbitrary element in a firm's own reckoning of its own depreciation allowances, and hence of its own profits, taxes on profits cannot be assessed on what firms themselves declare their profits to be; this would give far too much opportunity for evasion. It is therefore necessary for the government to lay down rules for the determination of depreciation allowances; the profits on which taxes are paid are calculated by deducting not the firm's own depreciation allowances, but the depreciation allowances laid down by law. Now it is these profits, calculated for purposes of taxation, which are recorded in the statistics used for calculating the national income on the income method; the figures given for the national income are therefore dependent to some extent upon the rules for the calculation of depreciation allowances which have been laid down by Congress and the Bureau of Internal Revenue.

Depreciation allowances, drawn up for the purpose of securing fairness in taxation, do not necessarily give us a satisfactory measure for use in calculating the national income. It is probable that in practice the discrepancy is not often serious; nevertheless economists have the responsibility of trying to discover the principles on which depreciation allowances ought to be calculated for this other purpose, in order that they should be on the look-out for such discrepancies as may arise.

It is not possible in this place to go far into the economic theory of depreciation, not all of which is well agreed among economists; two points which are well established nevertheless deserve to be mentioned. One is the distinction between depreciation and capital losses. When calculating the income or output of a year we have to deduct as depreciation the capital equipment used up in the process of production; but we should not deduct any accidental destruction of capital equipment which occurred otherwise than as a consequence of production. In the year 1941 a considerable amount of

British capital equipment was destroyed in air raids; a loss of this sort must not be deducted before arriving at the net output of the year, if only because the figure got after deducting that loss would be less significant than the figure for output without such deduction. It would be absurd to regard Britain in 1941 as having no output at all until it had produced enough to offset the air-raid damage! But it will be noticed that if we regard such losses as *capital losses,* not included in depreciation, then it is not necessarily true to say that the capital of the community at the end of the year equals the capital at the beginning *plus* net investment. The capital at the end of the year may be reduced below this level to the extent of such capital losses.

The official rules for calculating depreciation allowances make no mistake on this point; they proceed by allowing a certain percentage of the original purchase price of each piece of fixed capital equipment still in use during the year, and are thus under no temptation to include capital losses. But although it is necessary, in the interests of fairness, to go back to the original purchase price (for that is firm ground, not somebody's guess), to do this is *not* economically satisfactory. For the original purchase price of a piece of equipment is not one of the prices of this year; it belongs to an earlier year, sometimes a much earlier year; thus when prices are changing, the practice of reckoning depreciation allowances on this basis introduces a new complication into the problem of expressing the national income in real terms. When prices are rising, the fact that depreciation allowances are based on conditions as they were when prices were lower means that they may underestimate the real economic depreciation; the national income is therefore made a little higher than it should be. Conversely, when prices are falling, the national income may be made a little lower than it should be. American national income statistics are adjusted to offset this bias; but the adjustment (based on estimates of the age of equipment and equipment price levels) is unavoidably somewhat arbitrary.

A distortion similar to this last (but not identical with it) may arise on the side of working capital. If the community possessed exactly the same quantities of all sorts of single-use producers' goods at the end of the year as it did at the beginning, then clearly we ought to say that no net investment in working capital had taken place (apart from the possibility of capital losses). But if there had been a change in prices *during* the year, the value of the working capital would be altered; the accounting methods employed in practice would probably show this as positive net investment if prices were rising, and certainly show it as negative net investment if prices were falling.[4] In a more realistic case, with higher quantities of some goods at the end of the year than at the beginning, and lower quantities of others, it becomes hardly possible to conceive of a system of accounting which would not produce some distortion of this sort. Like the distortion on the side of fixed capital, this distortion on the side of working capital can be allowed for in national income calculations. It is to some extent a matter of taste whether one does allow for it; the compilers of the British White Paper changed their mind on the subject between 1941 and 1942, and this was the main reason why their estimate for the national income in 1938 came out more than £150 millions higher in the second White Paper than in the first. (The figure for Undistributed Profits had of course to be written up in a corresponding manner.) The year 1938 was one of falling prices.

During the war, changes in inventory valuation in the United States have been quite substantial, amounting in one year to not less than $3.2 billion. In general, the inclusion in income of profits from this source would tend to exaggerate

---

[4] There has frequently been a misunderstanding on this point. If stocks are turned over more than once a year (as is usual), some correction needs to be introduced even in the case of rising prices.

both increases and decreases from year to year, and has had
this effect in some published American series. Changes in
income-tax regulations to facilitate 'last in, first out' accounting of inventory are likely to reduce the statistical consequences of these changes for the future. The inventory valuation adjustment is not distributed as among industries or as
between incorporated and unincorporated business, so that it
is necessary in Chapter xiv to show it as a separate item rather
than present all the components of national income on a corrected basis.

NOTE D. *On What Is Meant by a Favorable or Adverse Balance of Payments*

The equation of the balance of payments, as we wrote it
on p. 165, states a necessary equality between two totals; the
difference between these totals is necessarily nil. Thus, when
a country is said to have a favorable balance of payments, it
cannot mean that the right-hand side of this equation is
greater than the left-hand side; for that is impossible. There
is, however, a useful meaning which can be given to the ex-
pression—or rather, there are two such meanings. They are not
always distinguished as carefully as they should be, but it is
important to distinguish them, for they have a very different
economic significance. One of them is concerned with the
strength or weakness of the foreign-exchange position, and is
thus of *monetary* importance; the other is concerned with the
contribution of external transactions to the accumulation of
capital by the nation within the period.

In the first sense, a country may be said to have a favorable
balance of payments (it might be better to say a *strong* balance of payments) if the bank lendings—and other temporary
lendings—which we have seen to come in as a balancing factor
if the other items in the balance of payments do not balance,
show a surplus in the direction of lending to foreigners; or if

there is a net movement of gold into the country. If there is a surplus of bank lending to foreigners, but an export of gold, then the surplus of bank lending must be greater than the export of gold; if there is an import of gold, but a surplus of bank lending in the other direction, then the balance of payments is still *strong* if the import of gold is the larger. In the contrary case, when the balance is in the direction of gold export, or bank borrowing from foreigners, the balance of payments will be *weak*. Serious weakness in the balance of payments is important, because it creates difficulties in maintaining the value of the nation's currency in terms of foreign currencies.

The other sense, for which the terms favorable and adverse are better reserved, is concerned with the balance of payments on income account. The balance of payments on income account may be said to be favorable if the country is adding to that part of the national capital which consists of its net foreign assets *plus* its gold stock. Thus a favorable balance of payments means that net imports of gold *plus* net savings invested abroad add up to a positive quantity. Referring to the equation of the balance of payments on income account, it will be seen that this can only happen if the total of home produce exported *plus* net income from foreign assets is greater than the value of consumption out of imports *plus* home investment out of imports (importation of gold not being included in this home investment). The amount of the favorable balance of payments is the difference between these totals; if the difference goes the other way, the balance of payments may be said to be adverse.

The existence of an adverse balance of payments means that the country is eating into that part of the national capital which consists of its gold stock *plus* its net foreign assets; but of course this does not necessarily mean that the national capital as a whole is being reduced. The loss on this part may be outweighed by a gain on the other part; that is, the adverse balance of payments may be outweighed by net investment at home. We have an example of this in the British accounts for the year 1938, which are described in Chapter xɪv of the British edition of this book. In that year the British balance of payments was very *weak;* the loss of gold appears to have been more than £200 millions. Most of this was due to the withdrawal of foreign funds which occurred at the time of the Munich crisis; in view of the political uncertainty, continental capitalists preferred to hold their assets in the form of obligations due to them by financial institutions in America instead of in England. Thus the loss of gold was offset by a diminution in liabilities to foreigners to a considerable extent; in so far as it was offset in this way, no net loss of national capital was involved. The only part of the export of gold which did involve a loss of national capital was the £55 millions, sold off by the government to pay for its armaments expenditure. This was the adverse balance of payments on income account. The things acquired with this expenditure are reckoned into the national capital; nevertheless the national capital was higher at the end of the year than at the beginning, not lower. The private investment in Britain (about £400 millions) more than offset the adverse balance of payments. The national capital increased during the year 1938, but its make-up changed. Real equipment at home increased considerably; net foreign assets increased (because of the reduction in foreign liabilities); the gold stock was considerably reduced. Changes in the gold stock are still very important; but the gold stock is necessarily a very small part of the national capital.

These are the two useful senses in which the terms we have been discussing can be used. Historically, they are descended from the terms favorable and adverse balance of *trade;* a favorable balance of trade simply meant an excess of exports over imports. As we have seen, it is of little economic significance whether a country's balance of trade is favorable or adverse. I have therefore avoided using the term balance of trade in this book.

NOTE E. *On the Place of Indirect Taxes in the National Income*

On two or three occasions, in the later chapters of this book, we have been obliged to skirt round an awkward and still somewhat controversial question about indirect taxes. First of all, we saw on p. 178 that if the national income, as usually measured, is to come out equal in money value to the real goods and services on which it is spent, those goods and services must be valued not at the prices actually paid for them in the market, but at *factor cost*—that is, at prices from which any indirect taxes charged on the respective commodities have been deducted. This is a tiresome complication, and it proves very inconvenient when (as in Chapter XVI) we desire to use the national income in real terms as a measure of economic progress. The index-numbers of prices which are available to us are ordinarily index-numbers of market prices, not of factor costs; [5] thus before we can use an index-number of prices to convert the national income into real terms, we must add the revenue from indirect taxes on to the national income as previously measured, so as to get a figure for the *market value* of the goods and services contained in the national income.

Now it is natural to ask: would it not be better to face this difficulty from the start, and to *define* the money value of the national income as equal to the market value of the goods and services contained in it—thus as equal to the national income (as previously measured) *plus* the indirect taxes? This is in fact what was done by Mr. Colin Clark (supported by the high authority of Professor Pigou) in most of his earlier cal-

---

[5] This is brought home when we notice that a rise in the tax on cigarettes (say) will ordinarily cause a rise in the cost-of-living index.

culations. The official United States Department of Commerce series of 'gross national product at market prices' goes still further and includes also depreciation. These procedures are convenient and therefore tempting; but (at least in the view of the present writer) they are not really satisfactory and must be rejected. It is only for this particular purpose of getting an index of economic progress (strictly speaking, of comparing the level of economic welfare reached in different circumstances) that we have to make this special addition of the indirect taxes. For this particular purpose, it is essential to have the goods and services valued at market prices—not only because of the nature of our price index-numbers, but also for a more subtle reason. We seek to compare the position of a representative consumer in one situation with his position in another situation, and the choices before him in each situation are indicated by the actual prices paid, not by the factor costs of the commodities purchased.

These market prices therefore lead us to the most appropriate 'weights' for measuring 'real' changes in total consumption; and, on the principles explained in Chapter xv, changes in 'real consumption' may be measured by 'deflating' consumption expenditure with the aid of an index-number of prices paid by consumers—in so far as consumption consists of goods and services actually purchased. (In so far as consumption consists of goods and services produced in the household, or provided gratuitously by government, the resulting measure is incomplete; and in times of rapid social change or of sharp fluctuations in business activity its degree of completeness may change deceptively.) In measuring changes in investment, market prices of investment also are better measures of the relative importance placed on different goods than are their factor costs; though for a number of reasons even market prices yield much less satisfactory 'weights' for investment than for consumption.

Measures of changes in 'real social output,' combining

consumption, investment, and government, are a degree less satisfactory again. As was noted in Chapter XIII, we should need for this purpose to be able to sort out the government services which are direct contributions to consumers' welfare from those which assist industrial production, and available figures are only makeshifts. A good price index for 'deflating' the current value of government services can scarcely be found; and the weighting system required for combining the three components is hard to work out. On the other hand, it must be remembered that consumption makes up the great bulk of social output, so that most of the weight in the price index used for deflating national income rests on the consumption component. We know also that the prices of new equipment tend to change in the same direction as those of consumption goods; and the same is presumably true of the prices we should ascribe to government services, since the cost of carrying out specified tasks (such as protection against fire) depends largely on wage rates and market prices of equipment and supplies. Consequently, for comparisons of years close together we can be confident that we are avoiding gross error if the price index used to deflate the national income in measuring changes in 'real' social product does not diverge very sharply from the index of prices paid by consumers.

For all purposes other than measuring changes in the total size of 'real' social product, the national income at factor cost is the more important magnitude. For example, if we wish to get an idea of the division of the national income between capital and labor (as we did in Chapter XIV) or between rich and poor (as we did in Chapter XVII), it is the proportion of the nation's resources which is devoted to satisfying the wants of each class that is what matters—and this proportion is shown by the measurement in terms of factor cost. A simple example will make this clear. Suppose that rich people spent all their surplus incomes on whisky, which is very heavily taxed. Their total expenditure might be very large; but if they were to be deprived of the means of making this expenditure only a very limited amount of resources would be set free to satisfy the wants of more abstemious people. The principal result would be a considerable loss of revenue to the government from the duty on spirits; that loss would have to be made up before anything was available to be used for other purposes.

This argument applies not only to questions of the redistribution of income, but to all other uses of the national-income accounts, excepting that particular use for the purpose of comparing economic welfare in different circumstances, with which we were concerned in Chapter xvi—and with which, it is fair to say, Professor Pigou and Mr. Clark were also mainly concerned. It therefore seems that much the best solution is to use the definition in terms of factor cost as the basic definition, but to modify it by adding in the indirect taxes when we are concerned with the particular problem of comparing economic welfare.

More sophisticated arguments in favor of the same course of action are set out (though with different emphasis) in an article by the present writer, 'The Valuation of the Social Income' (*Economica*, 1940).

NOTE F. *On Comparison Between the Real National Incomes of Different Countries*

In principle, the same methods as those used in Chapter xvi, for comparing the economic welfare of the same country in two different years, may be used for comparing the economic welfare of two different countries. But the difficulties in the way of getting a result that means anything are far greater. The circumstances existing at the same time in two different countries may easily differ far more drastically than those which are likely to exist in the same country in successive years; for the purposes of such comparisons, even France in 1941 was more like France in 1938 than England is like the United States. These great differences in national circumstances make it necessary to pay particular attention, when making international comparisons, to all those defects of the national income as a measure of economic welfare which we listed on p. 210. National habits about the sorts of useful work which are paid for differ widely; the amount of effort needed for similar sorts of work varies with climate and national temperament; the proportion of the national income used for defense varies greatly within a nation as political circumstances change, but it varies between one nation and another for simple reasons of geography. Then the comparison of prices between different nations is a particularly intricate matter. It often happens that there are wide differences between the sorts of commodities which different peoples principally consume; this means that the basket of commodities consumed by a representative (say) Italian will nearly always cost more in England than it would in Italy, but at the same time the basket of commodities consumed by an Englishman would cost more in Italy than it would in England. Are we then to say that prices are higher in Italy than in England, or vice versa? We can probably arrive at a moderately satisfactory answer by some device for splitting the difference; the result thus reached may have some meaning, but we should be unwise to place more than a limited amount of confidence in it.

Even if all these difficulties can be overcome—and with care (which is not always taken) they can be overcome more or less—there is still the fundamental difficulty that people who live in favorable geographical circumstances acquire freely all sorts of things which others have to earn by the sweat of the brow. Those who live in cold climates need more fuel, more clothing, and probably even more food, than those whose allowance of free sunshine is more generous. This is not at all to deny that there are poor nations and rich nations, just as there are poor and rich people within a nation. Their existence is obvious; international inequalities create social problems as grave, or graver, than the inequalities of class. The warning is concerned with a limitation of economics; what economics has to say about the comparison between the economic welfare attained by the same person (or similar persons) in different economic circumstances is almost illimitable; but comparisons between people who differ in other important respects are a much more slippery matter.